# The Sower Went Out to Sow

# The Sower Went Out to Sow

by

## Terry Barge

DAGMAR
MIURA
LOS ANGELES

The Sower Went Out to Sow

For more information, you can contact the author at terrybarge1@gmail.com.

First published 2024

ISBN:   979-8-89195-021-4

# Contents

"But speaking the truth in love, we will grow to become in every respect the mature body of him who is the head, that is, Christ. From him, the whole body joined and held together by every supporting ligament, grows, and builds itself up in love, as each part does its work." (Ephesians 4:15)

# Foreword

In early 2023, I felt a strong and definite urging by the Holy Spirit to re-examine several of my Christian beliefs and several spiritual truths and review what I considered the guiding principles of my spiritual life. It was an absolute necessity to ask the Holy Spirit to guide me on this journey and bring to my attention those beliefs and principles that He wanted me to research and review, and what happened thereafter, turned into a veritable voyage of discovery that lasted for about six months.

In my secular career as a sales and marketing consultant and strategist, I have travelled extensively and authored some books. So, it seemed that as I researched and reviewed, I could use that transferable skill and write up my findings.

The leading of the Holy Spirit was extremely clear and those truths that He wanted me to explore became very evident, one by one. During this time, I also created my group on Facebook, named 'Spiritual Food for Thought', and I posted what the Holy Spirit was showing me piece by piece. I also posted on my church's group page, 'South Chard Church' and I was also invited to join and write for another Facebook group, named 'Christian Community & Care.'

The urgency with which to research and review specific spiritual truths was extremely strong as was the motivation to write, it was a motivation and an urge that surpassed any normal or human enthusiasm. I knew it was the Holy Spirit, and I knew it was extremely important that I remained sensitive to His guidance.

The spiritual truths that appeared on my spiritual radar seemed to come 'thick and fast', as did the motivation to write up what I was discovering and post these pieces to the three groups. Those truths that the Lord guided me to examine, seemed to be 'anchoring points' for my faith. They were truths that would always secure me to Christ and enable me to live and function in line with His Will and Purpose.

At various times along the way, I asked the Lord whether I should compile my findings into a book. The response was a silence which I very quickly interpreted as 'Stay focused and keep doing what I'm leading you to do!' The voyage of discovery seemed to draw to a halt and that was the point at which the Holy Spirit seemed to say, 'Get the book done, I want the message out to my underfed and undernourished Church'.

So, that is how I ended up here, compiling this book from the truths I explored and the insights that the Lord provided to me at each stage. I believe this book can be used in several ways, but please see it as a starting point for your voyage of discovery, accompanied as I was, by the person of the Holy Spirit.

It is the Holy Spirit whose presence and leading are paramount whether you are just reading this book individually or maybe, using it in a group, as a guide to deeper study.

What I pray for you, is what Paul prayed for the church at Ephesus:

> "I do not cease giving thanks for you, mentioning you in my prayers, so that the God of our Lord Jesus Christ, the Father of glory, may give you the Spirit of wisdom and revelation in the knowledge of Him, that the eyes of your understanding may be enlightened, that you may know what is the hope of His calling and what are the riches of the glory of His inheritance among the saints". (Ephesians 1:16-18)

**Terry Barge – December 2023**

## CHAPTER ONE

# The Power of Choice

As Christian believers, we know that God is omnipotent, omnipresent, and sovereign. However, at the same time, He has placed an important responsibility for the choices and decisions we make into our hands. Because He's God, He already knows the decisions and the choices we will make at every stage of our lives, but those individual choices still must be made and are activated by an act of our will.

So, why does He give us the power of choice?

A choice is much more than just simply making a decision, about a situation that God has placed in front of us. Our choices represent a conscious act of our will, and as such, they demonstrate and prove to God, our preparedness and inner willingness to be obedient to Him, sometimes in challenging circumstances.

You may well be challenged as you read this book, and in some cases, you will need to make decisions and choices about what you read and what the Holy Spirit may well ask of you, as a result. In those situations, do not rush to either accept or reject. You should prayerfully and carefully, reach out to the Holy Spirit to guide you and reveal to you, how you should move forward. It may involve discussing your situation with other committed Christians whose spiritual insight and maturity you know, from experience, can be relied upon.

Isaiah summarised the essence of choice when it comes to the affairs of the Spirit:

"If you are willing and obedient, you shall eat the good of the land; but if you refuse and rebel, you shall be devoured with the sword; for the mouth of the Lord has spoken" (Isaiah 1:19)

We can choose to be willing and obedient, but we can also choose to refuse and rebel.

It is our responsibility to choose wisely.

> Jesus said "Here I am! I stand at the door and knock. If anyone hears my voice and opens the door, I will come in and eat with that person, and they with me." (Revelation 3:20).

Jesus knocks at the door but upon hearing His voice, the opening of the door is a responsibility which is very clearly left with us.

Joel underlines the whole universal scenario of human choice and decision-making:

> "Multitudes, multitudes, in the valley of decision!
> For the day of the Lord is near in the valley of the decision." (Joel 3:14)

Throughout the Scriptures, there are many examples of choices made and the consequences of those choices that were either enjoyed or suffered.

Whilst God instructed Adam and Eve not to eat of the tree of the Knowledge of Good and Evil, they still retained the ability to choose to obey or disobey, they were not created as robots, pre-programmed to respond to God like a television responds to a remote control. They had noticeably clear instructions from God but still made the catastrophic decision to disobey.

Joshua made his own choice, very visibly and very clearly, but he then challenged the whole of Israel to make a national decision to choose the living God, rather than the gods of the surrounding nations and those that had previously held them captive:

> "Now fear the Lord and serve Him with sincerity and faithfulness. Put away the gods your fathers served beyond the river and in Egypt. Serve the Lord. If it is displeasing to you to serve the Lord, then choose today whom you will serve if it should be the gods your fathers served beyond the river or the gods of the Amorites' land where you are now living. Yet as for me and my house, we will serve the Lord." (Joshua 24:14-15)

Noah chose to obey God and he and his family were the only

ones saved from the terrible flood.

> "Bring every living thing of all flesh, two of every kind, into the ark to keep them alive with you......
> Noah did this; he did all that God commanded him." (Genesis 6:19,22).

Abraham chose to obey God and offer up Isaac, his son, as a sacrifice:

> "Then they came to the place that God had told him. So, Abraham built an altar there and arranged the wood; and he bound Isaac his son and laid him on the altar, on the wood." (Genesis 22:9)

Daniel chose to remain loyal to God in the face of imminent death and was rewarded with deliverance from the lions' den.

> "Now when Daniel knew that the writing was signed, he went into his house. And his windows being open in his chamber toward Jerusalem, he kneeled on his knees three times a day and prayed, and gave thanks before his God, as he had been doing previously" (Daniel 6:10)

There was also a point in Jesus' ministry when some of His disciples decided to discontinue following Him while others chose to remain. When Jesus asked the remaining disciples if they were going to leave as well, Peter replied:

> "Lord, to whom shall we go? You have the words of eternal life." (John 6:68)

The disciples that stayed with Jesus made their decision as did those disciples that left Him.

However, not everybody made the positive decision that the loyal disciples made.

King Saul chose to disobey the commandment of God regarding the Amalekites and lost his kingship over Israel:

> "Samuel said to Saul, "I will not return with you, for you have rejected the word of the Lord, and the

Lord has rejected you from being king over Israel."
(1 Samuel 15:26).

Saul chose to reject the instructions given to him by God through Samuel and suffered the consequences.

The affluent, young man chose his material wealth and possessions over becoming a disciple of Jesus:

> "Jesus said to him, "If you would be perfect, go and sell what you have, and give to the poor, and you will have treasure in heaven. And come, follow Me." But when the young man heard this, he went away sorrowful. For he had great possessions." (Matthew 19:21-22).

He chose to place ultimate value in his wealth and possessions and not to follow Christ.

Demas, once a close friend and fellow minister with Paul, chose to abandon him:

> "Demas has forsaken me, having loved this present world, and has departed to Thessalonica…." (2 Timothy 4:10)

Ananias and Sapphira decided to lie to Peter about the proceeds of the sale of some land and the consequences were deadly:

> "Then Peter said, "Ananias, why has Satan filled your heart to deceive the Holy Spirit and keep back part of the proceeds of the land? While it remained unsold, was it not your own? And when it was sold, was it not under your authority? Why have you conceived this deed in your heart? You did not lie to men but to God. On hearing these words, Ananias fell down and died." (Acts 5:3-5)

By far, the most significant choice ever made though, was by Jesus, in the Garden of Gethsemane, who demonstrated, that as well as the Son of God, He was also the Son of Man. He showed that, as a man, He had to make the ultimate choice:

> "He went a little farther, and falling on His face,

> He prayed, "O My Father, if it is possible, let this
> cup pass from Me. Nevertheless, not as I will, but
> as You will." (Matthew 26:39)

It proved to be a most challenging but also a most obedient decision:

> "He went away a second time and prayed, "O My
> Father, if this cup cannot pass away from Me unless
> I drink it; Your will be done" (Matthew 26:42)

That same gift of choice remains with us today as it did with Jesus and many others, thousands of years ago. We are called to use that gift of choice wisely and comply with His Will and His Word throughout our lives. But it is still our choice and our decision to make.

> "I have set before you, life, and death, blessing and
> curse. Therefore, choose life, that both you and
> your descendants may live" (Deuteronomy 30:19)

## CHAPTER TWO

# What Is The Church of Jesus Christ?

Jesus said: "And I also say to you that you are Peter, and on this rock, I will build My church, and the gates of Hell shall not prevail against it" (Matthew 16:18)

So, what is the Church of Jesus Christ?

What was Jesus referring to when he spoke of building His Church?

Every Christian believer needs to understand what the Church of Jesus Christ is, and how they, as believers, personally relate and connect to it.

When you first consider what 'the Church' represents, you will get images of religious buildings, pews, hymn books, and pulpits. The problem with these images is that they represent a more modern perspective of what 'a Church' is and what its purpose has become.

This more modern perspective, though, is very much removed from how 'a Church' was defined by Jesus and throughout the New Testament.

It is also one of many indications of how far modern Christianity has drifted away from its roots and the true purpose of God together with a dilution of the truths and the doctrines set in place by the original apostles.

When you investigate the original New Testament meaning of 'the Church', you find that the original Greek word is 'ekklēsia'. The word 'ekklēsia' will again conjure up an English word like 'ecclesiastical' which will once more reinforce the same images as before, religious buildings, pews, and hymn books.

On closer inspection, however, we find that the modern usage of 'ekklēsia' is also far removed from its original Greek meaning, which is the original language of the New Testament.

The more accurate meaning of 'ekklēsia' is an assembly or a gathering of people. In ordinary Greek, it most often refers to the citizens of a city gathering to decide political issues and much less frequently to an assembly of religious devotees. So, for these reasons, the English words, 'a gathering' or 'an assembly' really work a whole lot better than the traditional word, 'a Church'.

So, when Jesus speaks of His Church, He is referring to the universal gathering or assembly of Christian believers. When Paul refers to the Church at Ephesus or Corinth, he is referring to the gathering or assembly of Christian believers in those two locations.

If you apply this more accurate definition of the Church being 'ekklēsia' to say, the Book of Ecclesiastes, you arrive at its meaning, which is 'a gathering or an assembly of wisdom' and very clearly, not the building in which the book is kept.

So, our more accurate definition of the word, 'church' means that any physical building in which the Church or 'the gathering' happens to take place is now, not so important.

Something else worth mentioning is that the number of believers constituting a church gathering or an assembly also is unimportant.

So, a Sunday gathering of a few hundred Christian believers is not the only accurate definition of 'a Church.' A Bible study group of thirty believers or a prayer group of ten believers, is also a Church – it is a gathering or an assembly of believers, in each of the three meetings.

When we speak about our 'Church', we are usually referring to our local assembly or gathering of Christian believers.

There's another interesting fact that reinforces our more accurate definition of the 'Church' as a gathering of believers rather than a physical building.

The earliest archeologically identified Christian church was a house church or 'domus ecclesiae'. This was the very first dedicated church building and was not constructed until between 233 and 256 AD.

In the early Church period and for some time after, there was no such dedicated building in which Christians met like a church as we know it today.

So early Church believers met wherever they could:

> "Every day they continued to meet together in the temple courts. They broke bread in their homes and ate together with glad and sincere hearts, praising God and enjoying the favour of all the people. And the Lord added to their number daily those who were being saved" (Acts 2:46).

You can also see that when persecution begins to impact the early church, it is the Christian believers who are attacked and persecuted. The persecution has little or nothing to do with physical buildings:

> "As for Saul, he made havoc of the church, entering every house, and dragging off men and women, committing them to prison." (Acts 8:1-3)

> "Now about that time Herod the king stretched out his hand to harass some from the church. Then he killed James the brother of John with the sword" (Acts 12:1).

A minister friend of mine once commented that the Holy Spirit had a real purpose in believers' homes being used as a place where believers could meet.

He suggested that it is quite difficult for family conflicts and dysfunction to coexist in the same home environment where prayer meetings and Bible studies are also going to take place regularly.

The pressure for family harmony and healthy relationships among family members becomes even more important when that home is also a meeting place for believers and, of course, the presence of the Holy Spirit.

However, there is another kind of building which is highly relevant and of significant importance to us all. It is not a physical building built of manufactured materials but a spiritual building, constructed for a very specific spiritual reason.

Stephen highlighted the nature of this building when

responding to the Sanhedrin after he was arrested and put on trial. He pointed to what was happening in Jerusalem, immediately after Pentecost, as a fulfillment of Isaiah's prophecy.

Isaiah had written:

> "However, the Most High does not live in houses made by human hands. Heaven is my throne, and the Earth is my footstool. What kind of house will you build for me? says the Lord. Or where will my resting place be?" (Isaiah 66:1)

What Stephen was stating here was that the Church, the gathering of believers, had replaced the Temple, the physical building, that Solomon had built. The earthly Church or the assembly of believers had now become God's spiritual residency. This Holy Spirit-inspired declaration of Stephen's becomes the first tangible evidence of Jesus' words when He said, "I will build my Church".

The Temple, which represented The Old Covenant, had now been superseded by the Church which represents the New Covenant. A key point to note here is that this is where the construction of the Church, that Jesus referred to, commenced. That construction has continued for the last two thousand years, from that point up to today.

There is only one universal Church of Jesus Christ and that is the one that He has been building over that period. It is a universal community or gathering of all born-again believers from that point in time until the present day.

So where do we, the modern-day believers, fit into this picture? Peter identifies our position like this:

> "Come to Him then, to that Living Stone which men tried and threw away, but which is chosen and precious in God's sight. Come and, like living stones, be yourselves built a spiritual house, for a holy dedicated and consecrated priesthood, to offer up those spiritual sacrifices that are acceptable and pleasing to God through Jesus Christ" (1 Peter 2: 4,5 Amplified)

Unlike the original temple that Solomon built of natural

materials as a temporary residence for God, this spiritual house, the Church, is built of 'living stones'. Those 'living' stones are those of us who are born-again believers who have been made alive in Christ.

Paul adds to Peter's comments, by highlighting Jesus' role as the Master Builder in overseeing the building of this spiritual house of God:

> "He is the head of all things to the Church, which
> is His Body". (Ephesians 1:23)

As well as being the 'head of all things to the Church' and the Master Builder, Paul also identifies Jesus in a much more specific way:

> "Jesus Christ Himself being the chief cornerstone,
> in whom the whole building, being fitted together,
> grows into a holy temple in the Lord" (Ephesians
> 2:19-21).

This 'holy temple', the Church, is made up of us who are the living stones, with Jesus as the chief cornerstone.

What is the significance of the chief cornerstone?

A cornerstone is the principal stone, usually placed at the corner of an edifice, to guide the workers in their course. The cornerstone was usually one of the largest, the most solid, and the most carefully constructed of any in the edifice.

The Bible describes Jesus as the cornerstone that His Church would be built upon. He is foundational. Once the cornerstone was set, it became the basis for determining every measurement in the remaining construction; everything was aligned with it.

So, we can see that the Church is of far more significance than simply being a physical building. The Church is God's permanent residence with Christ as the chief cornerstone and each true believer as a living stone.

Paul affirms all these key factors about the Church by describing the ultimate point when the Church will be finally built and completed by the master builder, Jesus:

He says,

"Husbands, love your wives, just as Christ also loved the church and gave Himself for her, that He might sanctify and cleanse her with the washing of water by the word, that He might present her to Himself a glorious church, not having spot or wrinkle or any such thing, but that she should be holy and without blemish." (Ephesians 5:25-27)

## CHAPTER THREE

# What Is The Body of Christ?

In Chapter Two, we covered valuable information about the Church of Jesus Christ. As we saw, this is the same Church that Jesus spoke about when he said:

> "And I also say to you that you are Peter, and on this rock, I will build My church, and the gates of Hell shall not prevail against it" (Matthew 16:18)

It is that same Church that has now become God's residence with Christ as the chief cornerstone and each of us, who are true believers, being the living stones. Paul described it like this:

> "...the whole building (the church) being fitted together, grows into a holy temple in the Lord" (Ephesians 2:19-21).

However, there is another important factor about the Church that we must understand. The Church of Jesus Christ is also known as the Body of Christ and is mentioned sixteen times in the New Testament.

Paul states clearly that these two definitions are synonymous:

> "He is the Head of all things to the Church, which is His Body". (Ephesians 1:23)

So how do these two definitions, the Church, and the Body, relate to each other?

The Church of Jesus Christ, which we covered in the previous chapter, is that spiritual community or gathering of which you, as a born-again believer, are a part.

The Body of Christ is how that spiritual community, the Church, operates and functions. We need to see then, that the Body of Christ is a living, breathing spiritual organism with Christ as its Head. This same Body, functions and operates, in much the same way as a human body.

So, am I a part of the Body of Christ? If so, how did I join? Paul again, explains:

> "For by one Spirit we were all baptized into one body. Whether Jews or Greeks or slaves or free, we were all made to drink of the one Spirit" (1 Corinthians 12:13 NET).

We were baptised into the Body of Christ. 'Baptised' means water baptism. The Greek word is very precise, and is 'baptizō', meaning 'to make whelmed, that is fully wet' We should, therefore, see water baptism as a profoundly important and significant commitment that applies to every Christian believer.

How do we function within that Body? Paul writing to the church at Ephesus describes it like this:

> "Christ has put each part of the church in its right place. Each part helps other parts. This is what is needed to keep the whole body together. In this way, the whole body grows strong in love." (Ephesians 4:16)

Paul clarifies it in an even more practical way when writing to the Corinthian church:

> "What should you do then, brothers and sisters? When you come together, each one has a song, has a lesson, has a revelation, has a tongue, has an interpretation. Let all these things be done for the strengthening of the church." (1 Corinthians 14:26)

So, while we are a living stone in the Church of Jesus Christ, we are also key members of the Body of Christ, called to personally contribute to its overall health and well-being.

What Paul is making noticeably clear is that we, as individual members of the Body of Christ, have a responsibility of love, to share and minister, so that we all grow stronger, together, as Christian believers.

So, how does that work? To understand how it works we need to be clear about the nature and character of the Body of Christ.

The character of the Body of Christ is built totally on a foundation of 'agape' love.

Agape love is that pure, unconditional love of God, demonstrated perfectly by Jesus and "shed abroad in our hearts by the Holy Spirit". (Romans 5:5)

Jesus set this culture of agape love in motion when he declared in John's Gospel:

> "A new commandment I give to you, that you love one another; as I have loved you, that you also love one another" (John 13:34)

God's love, agape love, continuously seeks to give and it is this love that we, as believers, are instructed to demonstrate with each other. Paul describes this love in action:

> "And let us consider one another to stir up love and good works, not forsaking the assembling of ourselves together, as is the manner of some, but exhorting one another, and so much the more as you see the Day approaching" (Hebrews 10:24-25)

He reaffirms this principle of God's love in action within the Body of Christ:

> "…that there should be no schism in the body, but that the members should have the same care for one another. And if one member suffers, all the members suffer with it; or if one member is honoured, all the members rejoice with it." (1 Corinthians 12:25-26)

So how are we equipped to demonstrate that unconditional love of Christ? As water baptism gave us entry into the Body of Christ, Baptism in the Holy Spirit empowers and energises us to share with and support each other, within the Body of Christ. As

Paul said to the Corinthian church:

> "The manifestation of the Spirit is given to each one for the profit of all" (1 Corinthians 12:7).

We will cover the Baptism in the Holy Spirit and the Gifts of the Spirit, in more detail, later in this book.

Paul emphasises this empowerment again when writing to the Ephesians and highlights, once again, how agape love is a key feature of how we are to contribute to one another:

> "But practicing the truth in love, we will in all things grow up into Christ, who is the head. From him, the whole body grows, fitted, and held together through every supporting ligament. As each one does its part, the body builds itself up in love". (Ephesians 4:15-16)

Therefore, while God chooses us to be 'lively stones' and to be a part of the universal Church of Jesus Christ, we are also called and fully resourced by the Holy Spirit to minister, share, and contribute to each other within that Church which is also, the Body of Christ. As Christian believers, we must fully recognise the significance of the Body of Christ and become clear about our part and role within it.

To move forward, we should fully embrace Peter's powerful and very timely exhortation:

> "The end of all things is near. Therefore, be alert and of sober mind so that you may pray. Above all, love each other deeply, because love covers over a multitude of sins. Offer hospitality to one another without grumbling. Each of you should use whatever gift you have received to serve others, as faithful stewards of God's grace in its various forms."

> "If anyone speaks, they should do so as one who speaks the very words of God. If anyone serves, they should do so with the strength God provides, so that in all things God may be praised through Jesus Christ. To him be the glory and the power forever and ever. Amen" (1 Peter 4:7-11)

## CHAPTER FOUR

# So, How Is the Church Doing?

S o far, we have looked at the true meaning of the Church of Jesus Christ and got a clearer insight into what that Church is, and, importantly, our place, as believers, in it. We have also looked at the meaning of the Body of Christ and, seen that it defines how the Church is designed to operate and how each of us, as members, is expected to function within it.

So how is the Church doing? How well is the Body of Christ functioning?

To gain that insight, let us step back in time and look at what was happening with God's chosen people, the children of Israel, when Jesus arrived to start his earthly ministry.

When Jesus arrived in Galilee, he found that the nation of Israel was spiritually, physically, and politically impoverished. This situation might appear to be very odd, at first sight. Israel is God's chosen nation about which the Scriptures declared:

> "For you are a holy people to the Lord your God, and the Lord has chosen you to be a people for His own possession out of all the peoples who are on the face of the earth". (Deuteronomy 14:2).

> "And what one nation on the earth is like Your people Israel, whom God went to redeem for Himself as a people and to make a name for Himself, and to do a great thing for You and awesome things for Your land, before Your people whom You have redeemed for Yourself from Egypt, from nations and their gods? For You have established

for Yourself Your people Israel as Your own people
forever, and You, O Lord, have become their God".
(2 Samuel 7:23-24)

What had gone so wrong for Israel? As a nation, here they
were, held captive in their own country, having been overrun by
the Romans. When Jesus arrived, Israel had already been under
Roman rule for around sixty years, and Roman captivity would
continue throughout his ministry and through the course of the
early Christian Church.

Their relationship with God was also wretched.

When the prophet Malachi stepped off the earthly stage around
450 B.C., no prophetic voice was heard again in Israel for about
five hundred years. The voice of God remained silent until John the
Baptist appeared, with his message of repentance and signalling the
imminent arrival of Jesus, the Messiah. Israel's spiritual state was
also, surprisingly, in a very dark place.

John the Baptist's message to Israel was very clearly one of
repentance from sin.

John spoke of repentance as a radical turning from sin. He
proclaimed:

> "Repent, for the kingdom of heaven is at hand. Pre-
> pare the way of the Lord; make His paths straight."
> (Matthew 3:2)

So, what of the Jewish religious leadership at that time?

Well, John the Baptist had a few choice words to say about
them when they turned up where he was preaching his message of
repentance:

> "But when he saw many of the Pharisees and Sad-
> ducees coming to his baptism, he said to them,
> "Brood of vipers! Who warned you to flee from
> the wrath to come Therefore bear fruits worthy of
> repentance and do not think to say to yourselves,
> 'We have Abraham as our father?' For I say to you
> that God can raise up children to Abraham from
> these stones". (Matthew 3:7)

Therefore, Jesus makes his Messianic appearance to God's chosen people Israel, a nation under Roman occupation, the religious leaders filled with corruption, the Jewish people in deep spiritual need, and the voice of God silent for five hundred years.

They were, though, a chosen people and a holy nation in whom God delighted. This blessing, however, carried with it a warning. There would be a consequence if they failed to honour God and keep his commandments. Through the prophet Isaiah, God had declared:

> "If you are willing and obedient, you shall eat the good of the land; but if you refuse and rebel, you shall be devoured by the sword; for the mouth of the Lord has spoken" (Isaiah 1:19-20)

Their catastrophic situation was a consequence of their failure to walk with God and keep his commandments.

While this was a very unfortunate situation for Israel, what has it to do with us as Christian believers in today's twentieth-first-century world? What has this to do with the Church of Jesus Christ?

We need to think about the current Christian world, as not being dissimilar to that of Israel's situation immediately before Jesus' arrival. We must reflect on where the Church is, in relationship to Christ's return.

To do that, we need to look at how the early Christian Church was established, the impact it had on the world around it, the degree of commitment of the early Christian believers, and the quality of its spiritual leadership. Then, we need to assess the degree to which the Church has fallen away from its original position and the current visibility of the initial, Holy Spirit-inspired doctrines and truths.

Remember that Paul declared:

> "Now, therefore, you are no longer strangers and foreigners, but are fellow citizens with the saints and members of the household of God, having been built upon the foundation of the apostles and prophets, Jesus Christ Himself being the chief cornerstone, in whom the entire building, tightly

framed together, grows into a holy temple in the
Lord, in whom you also are being built together
into a dwelling place of God through the Spirit."
(Ephesians 2:19-22)

Are all Christian churches preaching and demonstrating a full
Gospel as it was preached and demonstrated in the early Church?
Are today's pastors and ministers shepherding the flocks by teach-
ing those foundation truths that are pervasive throughout the New
Testament and designed by the Holy Spirit to build a resilient
Church containing strong, mature believers?

Are today's Christians fully committed to Christ and a disci-
plined walk with Him?

Is the Church filled continuously with the Holy Spirit? Is the
Body of Christ demonstrating the power of the Holy Spirit and the
gifts of the Spirit when it meets together?

Apart from a few exceptions, the global Body of Christ appears
in deep need of resuscitation and fundamental renewal.

However, there is incredibly good news. There is already a stir-
ring and an awakening underway across the Church of Jesus Christ.

As it was in John the Baptist's time, true believers are realising
that the time is short and have begun seeking God with a new hunger and a new commitment.

The Holy Spirit is working, and the Word of the Lord is truly
clear:

"Do not remember the former things, nor consider
the things of old. Behold, I will do a new thing,
now it shall spring forth. Shall you not know it? I
will even make a road in the wilderness and rivers
in the desert" (Isaiah 43:18-19)

As Christ appeared to Israel with a ministry of love, power, and
healing the Church is being called to rise again and embrace the
Lordship of Jesus and the infilling and power of the Holy Spirit.

Jesus' words are going to be fulfilled in His Church and through
His Body, across the world and in plain sight:

"Most assuredly, I say to you, he who believes in
Me, the works that I do he will do also; and greater

works than these he will do, because I go to My Father" (John 14:12)

## CHAPTER FIVE

# 'The More Excellent Way'

**D**uring his earthly ministry, Jesus made it noticeably clear to his disciples how they should behave towards each other. He said:

> "A new commandment I give to you, that you love one another, even as I have loved you, that you also love one another. By this, all men will know that you are My disciples if you have love for one another." (John 13:34-35).

Paul also regularly emphasises this necessity for love towards each other, in his letters to various churches, especially describing how that love should be demonstrated within the Body of Christ.

He stressed to the Corinthian church that they should seek to be always united and demonstrate that brotherly love by how they care and support each other:

> "......that there should be no schism in the Body, but that the members should have the same care for one another. And if one member suffers, all the members suffer with it; or if one member is honoured, all the members rejoice with it." (1 Corinthians 12:25-26)

He also emphasises to the Hebrew church that this love should also be seen in our regular fellowship together and how we need to spend that time in the mutual encouragement and edification of each other:

> "And let us consider one another in order to stir up love and good works, not forsaking the assembling

of ourselves together, as is the manner of some, but exhorting one another, and so much the more as you see the Day approaching" (Hebrews 10:24-25)

So, we can begin to see, that the spiritual culture of the Body of Christ is love, God's love, or 'agape' love. This is not human love or 'philia' love, which is brotherly love or friendship, but the unconditional, perfect love with which God loves us, 'agape' love.

Paul encourages us:

"But above all these things put on (agape) love, which is the bond of perfection." (Colossians 3:14)

We also know that the essence of God Himself is agape love:

"Beloved, let us love one another, for love is of God, and everyone who loves is born of God and knows God. Anyone who does not love does not know God, for God is love" (1 John 4:7-8).

It is this kind of love that Jesus instructed his disciples, and now us in the Body of Christ, to embrace and practice. So, how did we see this agape love demonstrated in the early Church?

Tertullian, the first Christian author and historian describes life in the early Church like this:

"But it is mainly the deeds of love so noble that lead many to put a brand upon us. See, they say, how they love one another……. how they are ready to die for one another." (Tertullian 197 AD)

Those 'noble deeds' that Tertullian described were demonstrated in a very visible and practical way in that early Church:

"All the believers were together and had everything in common. They sold property and possessions to give to anyone who had need. Every day they continued to meet together in the temple courts. They broke bread in their homes and ate together with glad and sincere hearts, praising God and enjoying the favour of all the people" (Acts 2:44-47)

We can already sense that agape love, as demonstrated in the early Church has a completely different outlook to human, philia love. Agape love is outward-looking and seeks to give, share, and contribute unconditionally to others.

Paul declared in his letter to the Corinthian church that agape love is not, in any way, self-centred and simply does not give to get - it's selfless and it's unconditional:

> "Love suffers long and is kind; love envies not; love flaunts not itself and is not puffed up, does not behave itself improperly, seeks not its own, is not easily provoked, thinks no evil." (1 Corinthians 13:4-5)

Paul affirms this again when writing to the Galatian church:

> "Therefore, as we have the opportunity, let us do good to all people, especially to those who are of the household of faith." (Galatians 6:12)

The good news is, that as true Christian believers, we can love, in the agape way, just as they did in the early Church. We can access and draw on agape love, God's love and, as such, go beyond the human limitations of philia love. Paul confirms this, writing to the Romans:

> "Now hope does not disappoint, because the love of God has been poured out in our hearts by the Holy Spirit who was given to us" (Romans 5:5)

John adds beautifully to Paul's words:

> "God is love. Whoever lives in love lives in God, and God in him. In this way, God's love is perfected in us, so that we may have boldness on the Day of Judgment, because as He is, so are we in this world." (1 John 4:16-17)

The same Holy Spirit that energised the early Church can and will energise each one of us as we submit to the will and purpose of God.

"...... that Christ may dwell in your hearts through faith; that you, being rooted and grounded in love, may be able to comprehend with all saints what is the breadth and length and depth and height, and to know the love of Christ which surpasses knowledge; that you may be filled with all the fullness of God." (Ephesians 3:18)

## CHAPTER SIX

# The Church – Political or Spiritual?

One of the biggest misunderstandings made by the Jews about Jesus' ministry was that they believed that he had come to release them from the Roman occupiers and replace the evil tyrannical, Herod Agrippa.

In other words, he was, like many before him, a chosen political leader of Israel who would set them free from political and military bondage, like Moses or maybe even David.

Even Jesus' disciples were still asking him, immediately before his ascension, "Lord, will You at this time restore the kingdom to Israel?"

They still lacked the insight about his true mission which was not at all political, but spiritual.

The only political statements Jesus made, were probably calling Herod, "an old fox" and telling people to "render to Caesar those things that are Caesar's and to God, those things that are God's".

His mission remained always, and, spiritual, and never political. He declared that very specifically when he repeated Isaiah's prophecy about himself:

> "The Spirit of the Lord is upon me because he has anointed me to bring good news to the poor. He has sent me to proclaim release to the captives and recovery of sight to the blind, to let the oppressed go free, to proclaim the year of the Lord's favour" (Luke 4:18-19).

Whilst we live today in a world that is highly charged politically, the mission of today's Christian church is no different from

Jesus' mission. Jesus set that mission in place when he said:

> "And He said to them, "Go into all the world
> and preach the Gospel to every creature. He who
> believes and is baptized will be saved, but he who
> does not believe will be condemned". (Mark 16:15)

The Church's mission is not political in focus but spiritual.

The early Church focused on that mission exclusively and, consequently, directly impacted the political world by the complete Gospel they faithfully preached and demonstrated. Theirs was a spiritual mission and never a political one.

The Church suffered consistent persecution from the political world, but never indulged or participated in any political activities whatsoever. In the face of intense political pressure and aggression, they remained faithful to their core mission, preaching the Gospel of Jesus Christ exclusively.

We see an example of the kind of political and religious pressure and violence they faced when it erupted in Thessalonica, following the preaching of the Gospel:

> "But the Jews who were not persuaded, becoming
> envious, took some of the evil men from the mar-
> ketplace, and gathering a mob, set all the city in an
> uproar and attacked the house of Jason, and sought
> to bring them out to the people. But when they did
> not find them, they dragged Jason and some breth-
> ren to the rulers of the city, crying out, "These who
> have turned the world upside down have come
> here too. Jason has harboured them, and these are
> all acting contrary to the decrees of Caesar, saying
> there is another king—Jesus.". (Acts 17: 5-7)

So, what should the Church's attitude and approach be to the present and aggressive political world if the focus of its mission remains the preaching and demonstration of the Gospel of Christ?

Paul is quite clear about what the scope of our Christian 'political considerations' should be. In his letter to Timothy, he states:

> "First of all, then, I urge that supplications, prayers,

intercessions, and thanksgivings be made for all people, for kings and all who are in high positions, that we may lead a peaceful and quiet life, godly and dignified in every way. This is good, and it is pleasing in the sight of God our Saviour, who desires all people to be saved and to come to the knowledge of the truth" (1 Timothy 2:1-4)

## CHAPTER SEVEN

# The Gospel Is the Power of God

In previous chapters, we have explored some of the truths that relate to the Church of Jesus Christ and the corresponding role and function of the Body of Christ.

We have also begun to look at how the early Church operated, demonstrating the unconditional love of Christ and focusing on its great mission, by proclaiming the complete Gospel message to the world.

We have also looked at the status of today's Church and observed that, apart from a few exceptions, the global Body of Christ appears in deep need of resuscitation and fundamental renewal.

One of the most incredible phenomena of recent times though is, the apparent ignoring by many church leaders of the miraculous and supernatural qualities of the Gospel message demonstrated by Jesus during his earthly ministry and throughout the early Church.

You could be forgiven for believing that they and many in the current Christian world, have never studied their Bibles, have little or no understanding of the full Gospel of Christ, or possess any insight as to how the early Church operated.

You feel that if the apostles were able to visit the Church right now, they would be horrified by how the Gospel message and the operation of the Body of Christ have both been corrupted and diluted, almost beyond recognition.

There seem to be two main groups of Christian leaders and ministers who have either wilfully or erroneously downsized the Gospel to just a spoken or preached word.

Firstly, some teach that the supernatural elements of the Gospel were removed by God once the early Church apostles died.

Their uninformed belief is that the apostles and the supernatural and miraculous elements of the Gospel they preached were simply to 'get the Church started'.

They go on to say that once the early Church was established, the 'with signs following' Gospel was no longer needed. God withdrew it, they say, because this more complete Gospel was no longer needed to substantiate the Gospel story in today's modern world; the written Bible record is quite sufficient.

Of course, along with this fully downsized Gospel, they also argue that the gifts and ministries of the Holy Spirit, initiated on the Day of Pentecost and covered so fully by Paul are also no longer needed to edify and build up the Church.

So, every element of what could be considered supernatural has been extracted by them from the Church and the Gospel message. In other words, all those elements and resources that the Holy Spirit has made available to the Church and distinguish it totally in the world from all other religions are apparently, no longer available.

We could well describe this group as the modern-day, Pharisees and Sadducees. The similarities are striking. See how their religious predecessors failed to recognise Jesus as the true Messiah even though they were Israel's religious leaders and steeped in the Scriptures.

In today's Christian world, these same 'Pharisees and Sadducees' fail to recognise the true and complete Gospel of Christ, even though, they too are Christian leaders and also steeped in the Scriptures.

Paul's warning is clear to those who would meddle with, adapt, or downsize the Gospel of Jesus Christ:

> "Although if we or an angel from heaven preach any other Gospel to you than the one, we have preached to you, let him be accursed. As we said before, so I say now again: If anyone preaches any other Gospel to you than the one you have received, let him be accursed" (Galatians 1:8-9)

The second group is those who feel the Gospel needs to be 'adjusted' to better suit the needs of a current 'culture' and be more palatable to modern-day intellects and values.

They take the view that the early Church existed around two thousand years ago and the culture that existed then has moved on and changed and the Gospel needs to recognise that evolution and be adjusted accordingly.

So, we see that whilst they may minister an adapted Gospel that might sound somewhat plausible, it is always going to lack any of the Gospel components that were so evident in Christ's ministry and the early Church.

The miraculous and the supernatural, although they may well be acknowledged, will never be actively preached, and certainly not acted upon. So, the lost remain lost, the sick stay sick, the captives remain bound and the demon-possessed still need deliverance.

In this instance, we do not see a downsized Gospel; we see a seriously diluted and weakened Gospel.

Again, Paul warns about this serious movement away from the true Gospel of Christ:

> "But I fear that somehow, as the serpent deceived Eve through his trickery, your minds might be led astray from the simplicity that is in Christ. For if he who comes preaches another Jesus, whom we have not preached, or if you receive another spirit, which you have not received, or another Gospel, which you have not accepted, you might submit to it readily enough." (2 Corinthians 11:3-4).

Paul's words to the Corinthians are quite stinging and he is scolding them and, taking them to task, with good reason. The Corinthians know the truth of the Gospel and they have experienced it as well.

Paul, though, is rebuking them for becoming lax and liberal and extremely vulnerable to being seduced by those who would introduce another Jesus, another Gospel, and another spirit.

Paul also warned the Galatians and that warning echoes down the years and needs to resonate again in the minds, hearts, and spirits of all ministers and every believer.

> "I am astonished that you are so quickly deserting him who called you in the grace of Christ and are

turning to a different Gospel— not that there is another one, but there are some who trouble you and want to distort the Gospel of Christ. But even if we or an angel from heaven should preach to you a Gospel contrary to the one, we preached to you, let him be accursed" (Galatians 1:6-8)

## CHAPTER EIGHT

# 'He Is Abba Father'

**B**y being born again we have become a member of the Church of Jesus Christ and by being baptised, we have become a part of the Body of Christ. However, another incredible thing has also taken place. We have been adopted into the family of God and He, Himself has become our Heavenly Father. John writes:

> "Yet to all who received Him, He gave the power to become sons of God, to those who believed in His name, who were born not of blood, nor of the will of the flesh, nor of the will of man, but of God" (John 1:12-13)

Paul explains it this way:

> "Now, therefore, you are no longer strangers and foreigners, but are fellow citizens with the saints and members of the household of God" (Ephesians 2:19)

The consequence of our spiritual rebirth is that, by a supernatural act of the Holy Spirit, we have left behind our old, corrupt way of life and entered a brand-new life in Christ. Paul writing to the church in Corinth says:

> "Therefore, if any man is in Christ, he is a new creature. Old things have passed away. Look, all things have become new." (2 Corinthians 5:17)

Paul again:

> "He predestined us to adoption as sons to Himself through Jesus Christ according to the good pleasure of His will" (Ephesians 1:9).

We have been transferred into many distinct aspects of the Kingdom of God – the Church, The Body, and now The Family of God!

We should be clear here that it is a combination of the Will of God, salvation through Christ, and the work of the Holy Spirit that have each come together to bring this incredible adoption process to fulfilment. With this in mind, we, therefore, need to reflect on just how especially important our salvation is to God Himself.

We need to ponder the supreme level of love and compassion He has for each of us in adopting us as children into His family and enabling us to genuinely call Him, Father.

We must fully understand the true significance of our new situation in the family of God and the true meaning of God being our Father.

That understanding and meaning are particularly highlighted in three references to God as not just 'Father,' but 'Abba Father'.

Jesus said in the Garden of Gethsemane:

> "Abba, Father, all things are possible for You. Remove this cup from Me; yet not what I will, but what You will." (Mark 14:36)

What was the true significance of 'Abba Father' here rather than simply 'Father', especially at this most critical stage of His life and ministry? Many have commented that 'Abba' is a much more intimate and endearing reference to God as a Father. It has also been suggested that Abba Father is more akin to 'Daddy' or 'Papa'.

'Abba' is certainly filled with intimacy and love, but also has another particularly important meaning which takes it beyond the childlike 'Daddy' or 'Papa' to a much more mature and adult emphasis.

'Abba', is certainly a term of intimacy and reflects a very close relationship, but it also carries with it a much deeper sense of obedience and compliance.

Jesus was praying intensely and intimately to His Father in the Garden, yet at the same time, He also expressed his submission to His Father's will. That is why he prayed, "Abba."

He displayed true and determined obedience to the Father

derived from the deep intimacy of their relationship.

He said:

> "My Father and I are one." (John 10:30)

Paul then highlights this important reference to 'Abba Father' in his letter to the Galatians:

> "But when the fullness of time came, God sent forth His Son, born from a woman, born under the law, to redeem those who were under the law, that we might receive the adoption as sons. And because you are sons, God has sent forth into our hearts the Spirit of His Son, crying, "Abba, Father!" (Galatians 4:4-6)

So here we see that our position as sons within the family of God means we have received that same Spirit as Christ. Paul highlights this point again, writing to the church in Rome:

> "For you have not received the spirit of slavery again to fear. But you have received the Spirit of adoption, by whom we cry, "Abba, Father" (Romans 8:15)

That same Spirit that lives within us, combines that same intimacy and obedience to God, our Father, with the intimacy and obedience that Jesus showed in the Garden. That is why He must be 'Abba Father' to us, because we too, have His Spirit residing within us.

Jesus never stopped reminding everyone of the importance and priority of the family of God and the need to have a personal and intimate relationship with God, as a Father.

He said of Himself:

> "My food is to do the will of Him who sent Me, and to finish His work." (John 4:34)

When the disciples asked Jesus to teach them to pray, He declared from the outset that they should regard God as "our Father." He positioned God, as a Father, and what is more, one who was superior to earthly parents:

> "If you then, being evil, know how to give good gifts to your children, how much more will your Father who is in heaven give good things to those who ask Him" (Matthew 7:11)

He demonstrated how much of a priority the family of God was compared to earthly, human relationships:

> "Who is My mother, and who are My brothers?" He stretched out His hand toward His disciples and said, "Here are My mother and My brothers!" (Matthew 12:48-49)

He emphasised this degree of priority of the family of God, even over our earthly, family relationships:

> "He who loves father or mother more than Me is not worthy of Me. And he who loves son or daughter more than Me is not worthy of Me." (Matthew 10:37)

He also emphasised this level of compliance and obedience to his disciples, so that they understood His full expectations:

> "Not everyone who says to me, 'Lord, Lord,' will enter the kingdom of heaven, but the one who does the will of my Father who is in heaven" (Matthew 7:21)

He saw the prioritisation and obedience to the will and purpose of His Heavenly Father as more than just supremely important, it represented the totality of His earthly life. He calls us to the same level of obedience to our Abba Father that He demonstrated:

> "For whoever does the will of My Father who is in heaven is My brother, and sister, and mother." (Mattress 12:37).

Paul reminds us of the level of commitment expected of us, as Christian believers:

> "I beseech you therefore, brethren, by the mercies of God, that ye present your bodies a living

sacrifice, holy, acceptable unto God, which is your reasonable service." (Romans 12:1)

CHAPTER NINE

# The Completeness of Christ

Jesus said: "I am the Way, the Truth and the Life"
(John 14:6)

This statement is one of the most powerful utterances ever made by Christ.

He positions Himself singularly and uniquely, as one of a kind, far and above any other spiritual leader or teacher. That singular uniqueness is that He declares that He is the only Truth, the only Life, and the only Way to approach and know God, enter His presence, and enjoy fellowship with Him.

What He is stating is that outside of Himself, there is no other route to God, no other access to His Presence, and no other way to enjoy the generosity of His love.

Outside of Christ then, there is no Way, no Truth, and no Life. Outside of Jesus, there is only a lifeless, spiritual darkness and spiritual death.

Christ declares that He is the only true image and the only expression of God that our human lives can ever know and truly experience:

> "No one has seen God at any time. The only Son, who is at the Father's side, has made Him known."
> (John 1:18)

Paul explains:

> "He is the image of the invisible God and the first-born of every creature. For by Him, all things were created that are in heaven and that are in earth,

visible and invisible, whether they are thrones, or dominions, or principalities, or powers. All things were created by Him and for Him." (Colossians 1:15-16)

Jesus said of Himself:

"Have I been with you such a long time, and yet you have not known Me, Philip? He who has seen Me has seen the Father. So how can you say, 'Show us the Father'?" (John 14:9).

The totality of our spiritual experience can only be found in Christ; and only in Christ is the totality of God, our Father. Paul states it very clearly:

"For in Him (Christ) lives all the fullness of the Godhead bodily" (Colossians 2:9).

As Christian believers, we are so blessed to be able to participate in all of Christ's fullness and completeness:

"Blessed be the God and Father of our Lord Jesus Christ, who has blessed us with every spiritual blessing in the heavenly places in Christ" (Ephesians 1:3)

Through grace alone, we have been elevated to an incredible spiritual position as a direct consequence of His redemptive sacrifice. Even more, our relationship with Christ was determined by God, long before the creation of everything:

"For those whom He foreknew, He predestined to be conformed to the image of His Son, so that He might be the firstborn among many brothers." (Romans 8:29)

Paul writes to the church in Ephesus:

"He predestined us to adoption as sons to Himself through Jesus Christ according to the good pleasure of His will" (Ephesians 1:5)

This fact is almost incomprehensible to the natural human mind. God saw us and set His love upon us before we even existed.

This incredible predestined and elevated position in Christ also means that we are totally blessed and fully provided for by His eternal supply.

Paul emphasises Christ's great provision:

> "But my God shall supply your every need according to His riches in glory by Christ Jesus. (Philippians 4:19)

We need to look no further than Christ for everything we will ever need. We have become true children of God and members of His royal family:

> "I will be a Father to you, and you shall be My sons and daughters, says the Lord Almighty." (2 Corinthians 6:18)

We are not only children of God but as members of His family, we also have an incredible inheritance in Christ:

> "…and if children, then heirs: heirs of God and joint heirs with Christ…" (Romans 8:17)

We have been given a direct and living connection with Him, via the Holy Spirit, every moment of every day. All that Christ is, has become accessible to every believer.

Jesus Himself said:

> "If you then, being evil, know how to give good gifts to your children, how much more will your Father who is in heaven give good things to those who ask Him" (Matthew 7:11)

Because of His amazing love, He directs us to fix our spiritual attention and energies on Him and He will provide whatever is needed for our spiritual journey. Jesus said:

> "But seek first the kingdom of God and His righteousness, and all these things shall be given to you. Therefore, take no thought about tomorrow,

THE COMPLETENESS OF CHRIST

for tomorrow will take thought about the things of itself. Sufficient to the day is the trouble thereof." (Matthew 6:33)

The Psalmist wrote:

"The Lord is my shepherd; I shall not want" (Psalm 23:1)

Paul encouraged the Philippians:

"Be anxious for nothing, but in everything, by prayer and supplication with gratitude, make your requests known to God." (Philippians 4:6)

As our Way, our Truth, and our Life, Christ has given us quite amazing access to all that God is and all that God has. By focusing upon Him and Him alone, we can have a great and unshakable confidence in His love, His support, and His provision:

"For I am persuaded that neither death nor life, neither angels nor principalities nor powers, neither things present nor things to come, neither height nor depth nor any other created thing, shall be able to separate us from the love of God, which is in Christ Jesus our Lord" (Romans 8:38-39)

## CHAPTER TEN

# 'O Wretched Man!'

When Adam and Eve disobeyed God and sinned in the Garden of Eden, they did not just destroy their relationship with God. They set in motion, a spiritual contamination that infected the human race from the point of their disobedience to the present day.

Humanity was, from that point, alienated spiritually from God and separated from His presence. The human race became sinful by nature rather than righteous, rebellious rather than obedient, and self-centred rather than God-centred.

David describes this alienated state:

> "I was brought forth in iniquity, and in sin, my mother conceived me". (Psalm 51:5)

David recognised that this alienated state was a continuum of sinfulness, which was passed down from human to human, father to daughter, and mother to child without interruption and apparently without remedy.

Paul makes an almost identical point to David:

> "Therefore, as sin came into the world through one man and death through sin, so death has spread to all men because all have sinned." (Romans 5:12)

Some attempted to live godly lives; Enoch, Noah, Abraham, and Job were among a few noteworthy men that found some favour with God. However, that original and uniquely harmonious relationship that God so desired, for the whole of humanity, was seemingly broken forever.

Paul states it simply:

"For all have sinned and come short of the glory of God" (Romans 3:23).

It seemed that God's desire for a people to call His own, a family that He could love and bless was not going to happen. Even when He finally created a family, the children of Israel, they too fell victim to that same sinful nature of disobedience, initiated by Adam:

"But they and our fathers acted proudly and hardened their necks and did not obey Your commandments. They refused to obey and were not mindful of Your wonders that You performed among them. But they hardened their necks and, in their rebellion, appointed a leader to return to their bondage" (Nehemiah 9:16-17)

They, like the whole of humanity, suffered the ultimate consequence of sinfulness and disobedience: spiritual death and alienation from God.

"For the wages of sin is death" (Romans 6:23)

Paul also describes this terrible dilemma of struggling and fighting with the desire to please God, but constantly being overcome by his innate sinfulness:

"For I know that in me (that is, in my flesh) dwells no good thing, for the will to do what is right is present with me, but how to perform what is good I do not find. For the good I desire to do, I do not do, but the evil I do not want is what I do. Now if I do what I do not want, it is no longer I who does it, but sin that lives in me" (Romans 7:18-20)

So, is there a remedy for this inherited sinfulness? Are we destined to suffer the consequences of Adam's disobedience even though we did not eat the fruit ourselves?

Yes, there is a remedy. The antidote for sinfulness and disobedience exists.

Paul declares simply, but powerfully, what the ultimate and only solution is:

> "O wretched man that I am! Who will deliver me
> from the body of this death? I thank God through
> Jesus Christ our Lord." (Romans 7:24-25)

Paul points to Christ as the unique solution for sinfulness, the subsequent separation from the presence of God, and its outcome, spiritual death.

He states that solution very clearly:

> "God made Him (Jesus) who knew no sin to be sin
> for us, that we might become the righteousness of
> God in Him." (2 Corinthians 5:21)

Peter adds to Paul's words:

> "For you know that you were not redeemed from
> your vain way of life inherited from your fathers
> with perishable things, like silver or gold, but with
> the precious blood of Christ, as of a lamb without
> blemish and without spot" (1 Peter 1:18-19)

Even before Peter and Paul, John the Baptist was proclaiming:

> "Look, the Lamb of God, who takes away the sin of
> the world." (John 1:29)

So, what are we to do? How do we access the righteousness of Christ?

A rejection of our past sinfulness and the embracing of a new life of righteousness in Christ is exemplified by repentance and water baptism.

Repentance and water baptism are inextricably linked. They are vitally important steps of faith and obedience where we relinquish our old, sinful, and rebellious nature and embrace a new life and a new nature in Christ.

We access the righteousness of Christ by obedience and by faith when we repent and are baptized.

Peter's instruction on the Day of Pentecost was noticeably clear:

> "Repent and be baptized, every one of you, in the
> name of Jesus Christ for the forgiveness of sins,

and you shall receive the gift of the Holy Spirit."
(Acts 2:38)

The Greek word for 'repent' is 'metanoeo' meaning to 'change one's mind, to experience a transformative change of heart'.

Paul then adds a clear explanation of the purpose of water baptism:

> "Do you not know that all of us who have been baptized into Christ Jesus were baptized into his death? We were buried therefore with him by baptism into death, so that, just as Christ was raised from the dead by the glory of the Father, we too might walk in newness of life." (Romans 6:3-4)

These are the points where we put off the old life of sinfulness and alienation from God and put on a new life of wholeness and right living in Christ. It is where, by faith, we say 'Goodbye!' to the 'wretched man' and embrace, by faith, our brand-new life in Christ.

We will be taking a closer look at the importance of Water Baptism later in the book.

Paul describes his rejection of a sinful, self-centred life and the embracing of a new, righteous life in Christ like this:

> "Yes, certainly, I count everything as loss for the excellence of the knowledge of Christ Jesus my Lord, for whom I have forfeited the loss of all things and count them as rubbish that I may gain Christ, and be found in Him, not having my own righteousness which is from the law, but that which is through faith in Christ, the righteousness which is of God on the basis of faith" (Philippians 3:8-9)

## CHAPTER ELEVEN

# 'For Me to Live Is Christ'

**P**aul the Apostle understood the significance to him personally of the completeness of Christ. He also completely understood the significance of repentance and the embracing of Christ as his Lord and Saviour.

Paul had, before his conversion, been a violent and active enemy of the Church He had aggressively persecuted the early Christians and created havoc and mayhem among the followers of Christ, especially in Jerusalem:

> "Saul, still breathing out threats and murder against the disciples of the Lord, went to the high priest, and requested letters from him to the synagogues of Damascus so that if he found any there of the Way, either men or women, he might bring them bound to Jerusalem" (Acts 9:1-2)

After his conversion on the Damascus road, Paul grew to see that his earthly life needed to become one that was devoted to Christ. Outside of the will and purpose of God, Paul grew to see that there was absolutely nothing in life that was of any importance at all. He stated that clearly:

> "Yet indeed I also count all things loss for the excellence of the knowledge of Christ Jesus my Lord, for whom I have suffered the loss of all things, and count them as rubbish, that I may gain Christ" (Philippians 3:8)

He reemphasised this total commitment to Christ for a second time in his letter to the Philippian church:

> "For to me, to live is Christ, and to die is gain"
> (Philippians 1:21)

He echoed so clearly the words of Jesus:

> "If anyone will come after Me, let him deny himself, and take up his cross, and follow Me." (Matthew 16:24).

He reflects that same sensibility, in an exhortation to all believers:

> "I urge you therefore, brothers, by the mercies of God, that you present your bodies as a living sacrifice, holy, and acceptable to God, which is your reasonable service" (Romans 12:1)

So, how does Paul's declaration affect us? To understand how our walk with Christ should be, we should reflect on how Jesus lived his life. Jesus saw his own life as having two completely interconnected priorities. He had one priority which was his utter devotion to His Father and His Will and, a second priority, which was committed to ministering to and teaching those who were in great need. First, Jesus said of Himself:

> "My food is to do the will of Him who sent Me, and to finish His work." (John 4:34)

Then, we see how Christ's total commitment to the Will of the Father, also went together with the focus of His ministry:

> "God anointed Jesus of Nazareth with the Holy Spirit and with power, who went about doing good and healing all who were oppressed by the devil, for God was with Him." (Acts 10:38).

In Jesus' life, His priority, fellowship with His Father, flowed directly into His other priority, His outreach to and love and compassion for the needy.

Like Jesus, Paul also saw his Christ-centred life as having these two interconnected priorities.

One priority was his walk and relationship with Christ and the other was his ministry and love for the nourishment and the wellbeing of the Church.

On the one hand, he declared a total commitment to his journey with Christ:

> "I press toward the goal to the prize of the high calling of God in Christ Jesus" (Philippians 3:14).

On the other hand, he also declared his complete passion and commitment to the Body of Christ:

> "And let us consider how to spur one another to love and to good works. Let us not forsake the assembling of ourselves together, as is the manner of some, but let us exhort one another, especially as you see the Day approaching" (Hebrews 10:24-25)

The early Church also demonstrated these two Christ-centred and connected priorities. The Apostles declared:

> "We will give ourselves continually to prayer and the ministry of the word." (Acts 6:4)

They recognised very quickly, that their commitment and dedication to prayer and communion with God was a priority that was inextricably linked with the preaching of the Word of God and the message of the Gospel.

> "Believers were increasingly added to the Lord, crowds of both men and women so that they even brought the sick out into the streets and placed them on beds and mats, that at least the shadow of Peter passing by might touch some of them. Crowds also came out of the cities surrounding Jerusalem, bringing the sick and those who were afflicted by evil spirits, and they were all healed." (Acts 5:14-16)

Again, we can see here how their true fellowship and communion with Christ flowed directly into compassion for those in great need.

So, what of us as Christian believers in today's modern world?

Paul exhorts us today as he did the Church at Corinth two thousand years ago:

> "Be imitators of me, as I am of Christ" (1 Corinthians 11:1)

Paul writing to the Galatians says:

> "For as many of you as have been baptized into Christ have put on Christ" (Galatians 3:27)

He points to our union and relationship with Christ as our most important priority.

This is the foundation principle of our fully integrated, Christlike lives that then needs to be manifested into a love and compassion for everyone especially, the needy.

As it was for Christ, the early Church, and the apostle Paul, so it is for us.

This is how we demonstrate the completeness of the life of Christ into which we, as believers, have been immersed.

> "I have been crucified with Christ. It is no longer I who live, but Christ who lives in me. And the life I now live in the flesh, I live by faith in the Son of God, who loved me and gave Himself for me." (Galatians 2:20)

## CHAPTER TWELVE

# More About Water Baptism

**B**eing baptised in water is one of the most significant and visible expressions of our faith in Christ we will ever make. In the early Church, water baptism was consistently an integral part of the Gospel message and not an optional 'extra' with little meaning.

When Philip preached the Gospel to the Ethiopian eunuch in the desert, water baptism was a key part of his Gospel message.

Why else would the eunuch respond to Philip's message with:

> "Look, here is water! What can stand in the way of my being baptized?"? (Acts 8:36)

On the day of Pentecost, Peter's exhortation to the gathered crowd was:

> "Repent and be baptized, every one of you, in the name of Jesus Christ for the forgiveness of your sins. And you will receive the gift of the Holy Spirit."

In both cases, the Greek word for 'baptise' is 'baptizō' meaning 'to make fully wet' or simply 'to immerse in water.' Paul realising that the new Christian believers in Ephesus had only experienced John's baptism, insisted they be baptised in the name of Jesus.

> "Paul said, "John indeed baptized with the baptism of repentance, telling the people that they should believe in the One coming after him, that is, in Christ Jesus." When they heard this, they were baptized in the name of the Lord Jesus". (Acts 19: 4-5)

Each of these examples demonstrates the priority placed on

water baptism by the early Church.

So why is water baptism so important to our spiritual life and well-being today?

Paul used the example of the Israelites passing through the waters of the Red Sea as a powerful example of the important spiritual message that water baptism represents. The pursuing Egyptian armies represented the Israelites' previous life of slavery, bondage, and pain.

Their passage through the waters of the Red Sea was like an immersion, just as we experience it, in water baptism. The journey through the Red Sea then, represents a complete separation from their terrible captivity in Egypt and the subsequent journey into a new life of freedom, blessing, and prosperity in a land flowing with 'milk and honey.'

So, this core principle of turning away from an old life of sin and bondage and entering a new life of spiritual freedom and well-being is at the very heart of the meaning of water baptism.

John the Baptist's message of repentance to the people of Israel, which heralded the arrival of Jesus, also contained the requirement for water baptism.

Once again Israel's status at the time of John was a similar one to the time of Moses. Israel was under the heel of the Romans, their religious leaders were mostly corrupt, the Temple had been defiled and the people were in great spiritual and physical need.

Moreover, there had not been a prophet's voice in Israel for four hundred years since Malachi.

John's message signalled a new awakening and a message of hope for Israel in desperate times.

Water baptism performed a key role, enabling those Jews who heeded John's message, to demonstrate that they were turning away from their corrupt and backsliding ways. They showed that they were turning in a new spiritual direction, represented by the arrival of a Saviour and Messiah, Jesus Christ.

> "John went into all the country around the Jordan, preaching a baptism of repentance for the forgiveness of sins......saying 'I baptize you with water. But one who is more powerful than I will come,

the straps of whose sandals I am not worthy to untie. He will baptize you with the Holy Spirit and fire.' (Matthew 3:11)

So how does all of this translate into our personal, spiritual experience?

Paul says this:

> "Know ye not, that so many of us as were baptized into Jesus Christ were baptized into his death? Therefore, we are buried with him by baptism into death: that like as Christ was raised up from the dead by the glory of the Father, even so, we also should walk in newness of life". (Romans 6:4).

He repeats this message when writing to the church in Colossae:

> "In Him, you were also circumcised with the circumcision made without hands, by putting off the body of the sins of the flesh, by the circumcision of Christ, buried with Him in baptism, in which also you were raised with Him through the faith of the power of God, who has raised Him from the dead." (Colossians 2:12)

So, we can see that water baptism is a critical part of our spiritual experience. It proclaims, openly, our death to an old life of sin and our awakening to our new life in Christ.

It also announces our arrival into the Body of Christ:

> "For by one Spirit we are all baptized into one body, whether we are Jews or Gentiles, whether we are slaves or free, and we have all been made to drink of one Spirit" (1 Corinthians 12:13)

Someone asked a minister once whether they were saved if they had not been baptised in water. His response was very direct:

> "You're asking the wrong question", he replied, "You should be asking, 'Where is the water so that I can be baptised?'"

Water Baptism is that important.

Without it, our spiritual life and experience are incomplete.

> "Giving thanks unto the Father, which hath made us meet to be partakers of the inheritance of the saints in light: Who hath delivered us from the power of darkness, and hath translated us into the kingdom of his dear Son" (Colossians 1:12-13)

CHAPTER THIRTEEN

# 'Except a Corn of Wheat...'

> "Truly, truly I say to you, unless a grain of wheat
> falls into the ground and dies, it remains alone. But
> if it dies, it bears much fruit." (John 12:24)

When Jesus used this allegory, He was pointing to His death. He wanted to emphasise that He was in human form. Consequently, His divine life and the impact of the message He was sent by God to deliver, was constrained by His humanity.

He described Himself frequently in the Gospels as the 'Son of Man," to emphasise that humanity. As a man, he was limited by the same human constraints as we are -limited time, limited energy, and limited resources.

Paul explains it like this:

> "He emptied Himself, taking upon Himself the
> form of a servant, and was made in the likeness of
> men." (Philippians 2:7)

There was an entire world that ultimately needed to hear and experience the fullness of the Gospel message and gain access to the complete blessing that God wanted them to experience and embrace.

He used the example of the corn of wheat to explain how His death would also make it possible, for us all, to share in and experience His life and His relationship with God.

His point was that a corn of wheat, whilst it remains on the ear of the wheat, cannot produce more wheat, it essentially stands alone and is unproductive.

Within that same corn of wheat, is the potential to reproduce itself, but not whilst it remains on the ear of the wheat.

However, the corn of wheat is also a seed and contains the embryo of the future plant; all wrapped up in a tough, protective coat.

For that reproductive process to be activated, it must be planted in the ground, and then for the corn of wheat to become fully productive, the outer husk must die, releasing the life of the embryo.

Likewise, the pure, spotless life of Christ was contained within His human form and people saw it and heard it, but it could not reproduce itself while it was constrained by His human form.

Jesus' human form, that protective coating, had to die and be buried in the ground so that His divine, resurrection life, that pure, spotless embryo, could be released by God and made accessible to us all.

Paul explains it like this:

> "But if the Spirit of Him who raised Jesus from the dead lives in you, He who raised Christ from the dead will also give life to your mortal bodies through His Spirit that lives in you" (Romans 8:11)

The first example of that resurrection life being reproduced is in John's Gospel when Jesus appeared to the gathered disciples, after His resurrection:

> "When He had said this, He breathed on them (the disciples) and said to them, "Receive the Holy Spirit." (John 20:22)

They were the very first to receive His resurrection life, and what is incredible, is that the same seed of resurrection life that resided within Jesus also became resident in each of them as well.

Peter explains it this way:

> "… for you have been born again, not from perishable seed, but imperishable, through the word of God which lives and abides forever." (1 Peter 1:23)

The embryo of Christ's eternal resurrection life comes and resides within each of us when we accept Christ and are born again:

> "We have this treasure in earthen vessels, the excellency of the power being from God and not from ourselves" (2 Corinthians 4:6-7).

However, like the corn of wheat, we need to also die so that the embryo, 'the treasure' can flourish and be shared out from within us. That "death" is represented by the abandonment of our previous fleshly life which we lived, separated from God like the corn of wheat, alone and unproductive.

Paul describes "death" as our abandonment of everything carnal and fleshly:

> "And those who belong to Christ Jesus have crucified the flesh with its passions and desires." (Galatians 5:24)

He restates that same principle in writing to the Roman church, but this time, emphasising the role of water baptism, which we covered in the previous chapter:

> "Do you not know that all of us who have been baptized into Christ Jesus were baptized into his death?" (Romans 6:3).

Water baptism demonstrated our commitment to the abandonment of our previously fleshly and disobedient life. So, what is the overall purpose here that both Jesus and Paul are showing us?

Firstly, if we have been born again and been baptized in water, we are directed to abandon our old life which we lived without Christ, separated from God.

Like the 'corn of wheat', we have to 'die' to our old, carnal life and become 'planted' in the fertile soil of God's kingdom.

We need to completely understand this first step because as part of God's family, we are expected, like a corn of wheat, to become productive.

Being productive is how God is glorified in our lives.

Jesus said:

> "If you remain in Me, and My words remain in you, you will ask whatever you desire, and it shall be done for you. My Father is glorified by this, that

you bear much fruit; so, you will be My disciples."
(John 15:7-8)

This is our calling, that we bear a lot of fruit, however, first we need to die to our unproductive life on the 'ear of corn' and, begin to 'live' unto Christ, bearing fruit to His glory.

Jesus said:

> "You did not choose me, but I chose you and appointed you that you should go and bear fruit and that your fruit should abide, so that whatever you ask the Father in my name, he may give it to you" (John 15:16)

## CHAPTER FOURTEEN

# 'Sitting, Abiding, Walking' – 'Sitting'

**T**here are times in the scripture when certain descriptions or definitions of the same thing can appear, at first sight, confusing.

We looked at one example earlier, when we saw that the Church of Jesus Christ and the Body of Christ, seemed to be different things, when in fact they are essentially the same. What was different was the spiritual perspective that each description was taking.

A similar dilemma might exist when we look at three quite different positions that describe various aspects of our Christian experience. I call it the "sitting, abiding, and walking" position of every born-again believer.

Each of the three descriptions could well be viewed as being different. How can I sit when I am also walking? However, these seemingly separate spiritual activities can exist, simultaneously, in every believer's life, but what is different is the perspective that each definition takes.

Let us look at 'sitting' first.

When we are born again of the Holy Spirit, we move to a completely new spiritual address, and our spiritual location changes, dramatically. By the power of the Holy Spirit, we become located, positioned, and seated in a completely new spiritual environment.

Paul describes it like this in his letter to the Colossians:

> "He has delivered us from the power of darkness and has transferred us into the kingdom of His dear Son" (Colossians 1:13).

He states it again to the church at Philippi:

"But our citizenship is in heaven, from where also we wait for our Saviour, the Lord Jesus Christ" (Philippians 3:20)

Peter describes this move to a new location in even more wonderful language:

"But you are a chosen race, a royal priesthood, a holy nation, a people for God's own possession, so that you may declare the goodness of Him who has called you out of darkness into His marvellous light" (1 Peter 2:9)

So, the perspective taken here focuses on where we are spiritually located because of receiving Christ as our Lord and Saviour.

We have left one address, the kingdom of darkness, and moved to our new spiritual home, the Kingdom of Jesus Christ.

Paul then gets even more precise about our exact location within the Kingdom of Jesus Christ:

"But God, being rich in mercy, because of His great love with which He loved us, even when we were dead in sins, made us alive together with Christ (by grace you have been saved), and He raised us and seated us together in the heavenly places in Christ Jesus" (Ephesians 2:4-6)

By the grace of God, we have become part of the ultimate royal family and have joined His royal household.

We have not just changed our spiritual address; we have also become seated together with Christ Jesus in heavenly places.

Regardless of our human or natural circumstances, our spiritual residence is in heavenly places, and sitting alongside us is Jesus, Himself. We are now sitting together with Christ as a chosen member of God's holy family. Paul puts it this way:

"Now, therefore, you are no longer strangers and foreigners, but are fellow citizens with the saints and members of the household of God" (Ephesians 2:19)

Let us rejoice and celebrate our new location and our glorious position in Christ, seated in heavenly places.

In the next chapter, we will take a closer look at not just 'sitting' but also 'abiding'.

## CHAPTER FIFTEEN

# 'Sitting, Abiding, Walking' – 'Abiding'

In Part One we looked at the believer's spiritual location and position in Christ because of embracing Him as Saviour and Lord. Paul highlights this new spiritual address in his letter to the Ephesians:

> "But God, being rich in mercy, because of His great love with which He loved us, even when we were dead in sins, made us alive together with Christ (by grace you have been saved), and He raised us up and seated us together in the heavenly places in Christ Jesus" (Ephesians 2:4-6).

The Psalmist describes it like this:

> "He who dwells in the shelter of the 'Most High' shall abide under the shadow of the Almighty, I will say of the Lord, "He is my refuge and my fortress, my God in whom I trust." (Psalm 91:1-2)

One thing we need to remind ourselves of is that we occupy this heavenly position in Christ by faith, and by faith alone, Faith is what enables us to continually enjoy all the spiritual benefits of our new location, Faith enables us to 'abide' or to remain seated with Christ.

Paul highlights this absolute function of faith when he quotes the words of the prophet Habakkuk:

> "As it is written, "The just shall live by faith." (Romans 1:17)

He again reaffirms the importance of active faith:

"And without faith, it is impossible to please God".
(Hebrews 11:6)

So, while we experience our human life via our five senses, we experience our spiritual life in Christ, by active faith in God's Word. Jesus described it this way in Matthew 4:4:

'But He (Jesus) answered, "It is written, 'Man shall not live by bread alone, but by every word that proceeds out of the mouth of God.'

So, while our human life and our spiritual life coexist, they also constantly challenge each other.

Our human life is sustained and experienced through our five senses, by the air we breathe, the food we eat, and the overall care we take of ourselves.

Our spiritual life though, is sustained and experienced by hearing and exercising faith in the living Word of God. So, whilst we are 'seated with Christ in heavenly places', it's so important that we continuously exercise our faith, to enjoy all the benefits that emanate from that wonderful position.

It is our faith in Christ and the living Word of God that enables us to continuously 'abide' or live in and experience all the benefits of being 'seated in heavenly places in Christ Jesus.'

That is precisely what Jesus meant when he said:

"If you remain in Me, and My words remain in you, you will ask whatever you desire, and it shall be done for you." (John 15:7)

Here is a great example of remaining or 'abiding in Christ', especially in the face of extreme and contrary human circumstances:

"After they had laid many stripes on them, they threw them into prison, commanding the jailer to guard them securely. Having received such an order, he threw them into the inner prison and fastened their feet in the stocks. At midnight Paul and Silas were praying and singing hymns to God, and the prisoners were listening to them. Suddenly there was a great earthquake, so that the foundations of the prison were shaken. And immediately all the doors were opened, and everyone's shackles were loosened." (Acts 16:23-26)

Paul and Silas 'remained' in active faith, 'praying and singing hymns to God' despite their appalling circumstances and we can see that their active faith was rewarded most miraculously.

Their human senses and circumstances tried to tell them one story, but their faith in Christ told them a completely different story.

So, whilst the Word of God declares that we are seated with Christ in heavenly places, we only remain or 'abide' in the blessing that flows from that position by actively investing our faith in His Word and His promises.

Let us go back to Peter's words again:

"But you are a chosen race, a royal priesthood, a holy nation, a people for God's own possession, so that you may declare the goodness of Him who has called you out of darkness into His marvellous light" (1 Peter 2:9)

Paul and Silas 'declared the goodness of God' by refusing to abandon their faith in the face of their awful situation, they did not just 'sit', they 'remained' in faith, not just sitting but also abiding!

It was their active faith in Christ that enabled them to 'abide' and prosper and bear fruit to the glory of God.

Let us embrace Jesus' words in John's Gospel and not just 'sit' but also 'abide' in Him, His Word, and in His unfailing love:

"You are already clean because of the word which I have spoken to you. Abide in Me, and I in you. As the branch cannot bear fruit of itself unless it abides in the vine, neither can you, unless you abide in Me. I am the Vine; you are the branches. He who abides in Me, and I in him, bears much fruit; for without Me you can do nothing." (John 15:3-5)

## CHAPTER SIXTEEN

# 'Sitting, Abiding, Walking' – 'Walking'

In Part One we focused on our spiritual position in Christ as born-again believers.

> "But God, being rich in mercy, because of His great love with which He loved us, even when we were dead in sins, made us alive together with Christ (by grace you have been saved), and He raised us up and seated us together in the heavenly places in Christ Jesus" (Ephesians 2:4-6)

We have now changed our spiritual address and become seated together with Christ Jesus in heavenly places.

In Part Two, we focused on faith and its vitally significant role in ensuring that we remain seated with Christ and that we continue to 'abide' in Him.

We saw that although the Word of God declares that we are seated with Christ in heavenly places, we can only remain or 'abide' in the blessing that flows from that position, by actively and continually, investing our faith in Christ, His Word, and in His promises.

In Part Three, we are going to look at 'walking' with Christ.

This might seem a little difficult to process at first as the natural mind might ask, "How can I walk and abide and be seated at the same time?"

This question is a good example of what we highlighted in Chapter Fourteen; it has to do with perspective.

'Sitting' and 'abiding' both focus on our spiritual position in Christ, whilst 'walking' takes the perspective of our spiritual journey as we travel through our day-to-day human life, Paul highlights this perspective of 'walking' several times in his various letters.

In Ephesians 5:8 he writes:

> "For you were formerly darkness, but now you are light in the Lord. Walk as children of light."

In Colossians 1:10 he does not just talk about walking; he describes the characteristics and the qualities of that walk:

> "...... that you may walk in a manner worthy of the Lord, pleasing to all, being fruitful in every good work, and increasing in the knowledge of God..."

The original Greek word for 'walk' in both cases is 'peripateō' which means 'to regulate and manage one's life,' so we can see that the perspective we're taking is, in fact, all about how we conduct our spiritual lives, as we live our natural human life.

Whilst we are truly 'seated with Christ in heavenly places' and by faith, we are remaining or 'abiding' in that 'seated' position, we also must live, day by day, in this world and that is the 'walking' part of our Christian life and journey.

How do we do that?

Paul explains:

> "Therefore, we are always confident, knowing that while we are at home in the body, we are absent from the Lord. For we walk by faith, not by sight." (2 Corinthians 5:7)

What Paul is emphasising here is, that while we are living our human life, we are not physically in the actual, live presence of Christ.

As a consequence, our day-to-day experience of Him, His presence, and everything we need to live victoriously, is accessed by our faith alone.

Paul describes this way of Christian living when writing to the Galatian church:

> "If we live in the Spirit, let us also walk in the Spirit." (Galatians 5:25)

Interestingly, the Greek word for 'walk' here is 'stoicheo' and it provides a slightly different emphasis to 'walking' than we looked at earlier.

'Stoicheo' adds a 'how' we walk component, as it means to walk or proceed, in a more precise and measured manner as 'in a military rank.' The Greek word also adds another element to our walking and that is, that our daily walk with Christ should also reflect 'piety' and 'virtue'.

So, this 'walking' part of our Christian life is clearly by faith but is also one that we are exhorted to conduct in an orderly manner, and with great care, and one that must also demonstrate holy and pure living.

So, we walk in the Spirit, by faith, step by step.

We read in Chapter Fifteen how Paul and Silas, despite being in an appalling situation, did not 'walk' or behave according to what their human senses were telling them.

They were praising God and rejoicing, because they knew, by faith, they were in fact, 'seated with Christ in heavenly places', living in the Spirit, and walking in the Spirit, and the result of their great faith was miraculous:

> "Suddenly there was a great earthquake so that the foundations of the prison were shaken. And immediately all the doors were opened, and everyone's shackles were loosened." (Acts 16:23-26)

This is such a great example of 'walking by faith and not by sight'.

We have been called to walk and live our day-to-day human life by faith.

As Paul said to the Roman church:

> "The just shall live by faith." (Romans 1:17)

Everything that God has provided for us to walk and live in a manner, which is glorifying to Him, is accessible by faith in His word and His promises.

So, let us exhort each other, pray for one another, and believe God for one another, as Paul did for the church in Colossae:

"For this reason, we also, since the day we heard it, do not cease to pray for you and to ask that you may be filled with the knowledge of His will in all wisdom and spiritual understanding; that you may walk in a manner worthy of the Lord, pleasing to all, being fruitful in every good work, and increasing in the knowledge of God, strengthened with all might according to His glorious power, enduring everything with perseverance and patience joyfully". (Colossians 1:9-11)

## CHAPTER SEVENTEEN

# The Vital Role of Faith

I n previous chapters, we have stressed consistently the vital nature of faith in underpinning every aspect of our walk with Christ.

We know as believers, that our salvation and our daily walk with Christ are both dependent on us exercising active faith in Christ and in His living Word.

Paul writing to the Corinthian church, describes how important faith is, in our journey with Christ:

> "For we walk by faith, not by sight" (2 Corinthians 5:7)

The Greek word for 'walk' here is 'peripateo' meaning, 'to regulate one's life' or 'to conduct oneself', so our verse could be more accurately translated as:

> "For we regulate our lives by faith, not by sight'.

So why is faith such a vitally important part of our Christian experience?

Most importantly, God has established the fundamental role of faith in that He has declared that faith is the only way we have of accessing Him and knowing Him.

Paul emphasises this in his letter to the Hebrew church:

> "And without faith, it is impossible to please him, for whoever would draw near to God must believe that he exists and that he rewards those who seek him" (Hebrews 11:6)

Our faith plays the primary role in knowing God and walking with Christ.

Jesus provides an insight into why this is so:

"No one has seen God at any time. The only Son,
who is at the Father's side, has made Him known."
(John 1:18)

As we saw previously, our walk with Christ is a spiritual walk
and our human senses will provide little material help in this spiritual environment.

John again explains:

"God is a Spirit: and they that worship him must
worship him in spirit and in truth" (John 4:24)

Jesus further underlined this fact when He explained this spiritual environment, He used the analogy of the wind to explain the
nature of the Holy Spirit and how He operates:

"The wind blows where it wishes, and you hear its
sound, but you do not know where it comes from
or where it goes. So, it is with everyone who is born
of the Spirit." (John 3:8)

Therefore, we can only know, access, and experience the spiritual dimension into which we have been born again, by faith.

Faith is generated from our hearts, and then revealed through
our senses, Paul explains:

"… for with the heart one believes unto righteousness, and with the mouth, confession is made unto
salvation." (Romans 10:10)

As we embrace Christ by faith and enter the Kingdom of God
by faith, we are also called to live our daily lives by faith, moment
by moment.

The good news is that God has imparted to everyone, without
exception, a measure or portion of faith:

"For I say, through the grace given to me, to everyone among you, not to think of himself more
highly than he ought to think, but to think with
sound judgment, according to the measure of faith
God has distributed to every man." (Romans 12:3)

So, faith and the capability to use faith is the great leveller in the Body of Christ.

Every one of us has a measure of faith and every one of us can utilise that faith in our daily walk with Christ.

Our access to God and our walk with Christ is not a function of individual intellect or academic prowess, if it were, then only the clever and the well-educated would be able to access God and build a relationship with Him.

The early Church is a great example of believers, who were mainly simple, everyday people, whose faith enabled them to achieve great things for Christ:

> "And Stephen, full of faith and power, did great wonders and miracles among the people." (Acts 6:8)

However, these same early Christians were also viewed as uneducated and unqualified by the religious leaders of the day:

> "When they saw the boldness of Peter and John and perceived that they were illiterate and uneducated men, they marvelled. And they recognised that they had been with Jesus." (Acts 4:13).

They were though, men who were filled with faith and with the Holy Spirit and were, therefore, both capable and completely equipped.

In contrast, we should remember that Jesus was robust with those who showed little or no faith:

> "His disciples went to Him and awoke Him, saying, "Lord, save us! We are perishing!" He replied, "Why are you fearful, O you of little faith?" Then He rose and rebuked the winds and the sea. And there was a great calm." (Matthew 8:25-26)

When He saw Mary and Martha mourning the death of Lazarus, Jesus wept. He did not weep because Lazarus was dead but wept because of their lack of faith in Him to raise him from the dead.

Their lack of faith distressed Him deeply:

> "When Mary came to where Jesus was and saw
> Him, she fell down at His feet, saying to Him,
> "Lord, if You had been here, my brother would not
> have died. When Jesus saw her weeping, and the
> Jews who came with her weeping, He groaned in
> the spirit and was troubled" (John 11:32-33)

As much as Jesus scolded a lack of faith, he was also quick to applaud those who displayed bold faith.

The Roman centurion with a seriously sick servant is a great example of one who demonstrated great faith in Christ and in His power to heal.

The centurion declared boldly:

> "But speak the word only, and my servant will be
> healed" (Matthew 8:8).

Jesus applauded his strong faith:

> "When Jesus heard it, He was amazed and said to
> those who followed, "Truly I say to you, I have not
> found such great faith, no, not in Israel" (Matthew
> 8:10)

A Canaanite woman approached Jesus, pleading for her demon-possessed daughter to be healed.

Jesus initially appeared reluctant because she was not a Jew, however, she persisted:

> "Even the dogs eat the crumbs that fall from their
> master's table." (Matthew 15:27)

Jesus again applauded her great faith:

> "O woman, great is your faith. Let it be done for
> you as you desire." And her daughter was healed
> instantly." (Matthew 15:28)

As Christian believers, we are called by Christ to use our measure of faith regularly and boldly, like the centurion and the Canaanite woman.

We are no different from these two individuals. We must

constantly exercise our faith in Christ and invest our measure of faith continuously in His promises.

This is how we increase our inner spiritual strength and allow the Holy Spirit to nourish us and maintain our overall spiritual well-being.

The New Testament is filled with stories of individuals who exhibited great faith in God.

These individuals, both men and women, demonstrated unwavering trust and belief in Christ, in the face of adversity, doubt, and physical disability.

We too, are exhorted by John:

> "For everyone who has been born of God overcomes the world. And this is the victory that has overcome the world—our faith" (1 John 5:4)

## CHAPTER EIGHTEEN

# 'Using Faith, Naturally'

**W**e just looked at the role of faith and how essential faith is to our initial salvation and our continuing walk with Christ throughout our day-to-day lives.

Our daily lives continuously provide us with opportunities to use our measure of faith and access the provision of God in so many ways.

Whatever the nature of the situation we are facing, financial, health, family, or career, we know that Christ cares for and supports us as His children.

Paul says:

> "In everything give thanks, for this is the will of God in Christ Jesus concerning you." (1 Thessalonians 5:18)

At first sight, this exhortation of Paul's might seem especially challenging.

However, what he is emphasising is the whole meaning of 'walking by faith and not by sight,'

He is stating that God wants us to exercise our faith in the face of those difficult challenges and unpleasant situations that we invariably encounter, throughout our lives.

The Holy Spirit is looking for us to grow spiritually in these situations, and not be governed by the negative information being communicated through our natural mind and senses.

This is why Paul says:

> "We know that all things work together for good

to those who love God, to those who are called according to His purpose. (Romans 8:28)

It takes faith to thank God for those challenges and situations that we encounter in life.

We have the promise of God available to us, it is our faith, which brings these promises of God alive, in whatever situation we are facing.

We have God's eternal and unfailing promise:

"But my God shall supply your every need according to His riches in glory by Christ Jesus." (Philippians 4:19)

As Paul wrote to the Hebrew church, faith brings the answer to our need, even before we see it in reality:

"Now faith is the substance of things hoped for, the evidence of things not seen" (Hebrews 11:1).

There are many instances in the Scriptures of individuals whose view of life was far more influenced by their faith in God than by any influence coming from their natural senses and circumstances.

When David appeared on the scene at the Valley of Elah, the armies of Israel were in a state of fear and alarm because of the challenge of Goliath, the massive champion and soldier of Israel's arch-enemies, the Philistines.

He stood at an unprecedented height of around 9'-6", was well-trained, and was suited up in an incredible amount of armour and armed with an impressive range of personal weaponry.

His voice rang out across the valley, as he issued his challenge to the men of Israel's army:

"This day I defy the armies of Israel! Give me a man and let us fight each other." (1 Samuel 17:10)

The fate of Israel lay in a single man meeting Goliath's challenge and overcoming him in battle. If Goliath prevailed, then Israel would become the servants of the Philistines.

However, no one dared to emerge from the Israelite army to take up the challenge, not even King Saul:

"On hearing the Philistine's words, Saul and all the
Israelites were dismayed and terrified." (1 Samuel
17:11)

Although Israel had a rich history of God's divine protection
and many examples, of Him subduing their enemies, no one it
appeared, could muster enough faith that day to even respond to
Goliath, let alone fight him.

The very sight of the enormous Goliath caused them all to lose
sight of the greatness of God and become paralysed with fear.

Here we see a perfect example of how their natural senses
unduly influenced them to the point where they lost sight of God,
their faith evaporated, and they subsequently failed to access His
incredible provision.

David arrived on the scene by chance but was soon made
aware of Goliath's presence when he heard Goliath issue his daily
challenge.

He quickly responded and said to King Saul: "Let no one lose
heart on account of this Philistine; your servant will go and fight
him."

This astounding declaration by David was not just youthful bra-
vado but was grounded in his relationship with God and his experience of investing faith in God's support and help at critical times:

"Your servant has killed both the lion and the bear; this uncir-
cumcised Philistine will be like one of them because he has defied
the armies of the living God. The Lord who rescued me from the
paw of the lion and the paw of the bear will rescue me from the
hand of this Philistine." (1 Samuel 17:36-37)

Victory over Goliath was therefore inevitable to David - it was
already assured and certain, his faith in his God embraced victory
before it happened:

"You come against me with sword and spear and
javelin, but I come against you in the name of the
Lord Almighty, the God of the armies of Israel,
whom you have defied. This day the Lord will
deliver you into my hands, and I will strike you
down and cut off your head." (1 Samuel 17:45-46)

David walked by faith and not by sight and vanquished Goli-ath because he would not listen to his human senses but chose to put his faith in the power and might of his God which was more than enough to overcome Goliath.

Another prime example of walking by faith and not by sight occurred on the Israelites' journey to Canaan. Moses was directed by God, to send out ten spies to assess the enemy's situation:

> "Moses sent them to spy out the land of Canaan, he said to them, "Go up there into the Negev; then go up into the hill country. See what the land is like, and whether the people who live in it are strong or weak, whether they are few or many...." (Numbers 13:17-18)

However, when the spies returned from their mission, Moses found himself having to deal with two distinctly different reports. Eight of the spies reported:

> "We came into the land where you sent us, and it certainly does flow with milk and honey, and this is its fruit. Nevertheless, the people who live in the land are strong, and the cities are fortified and very large...... we are not able to go up against the peo-ple, because they are too strong for us" (Numbers 13:27-28,31)

However, two of the spies, Joshua, and Caleb, observed the same things but had a completely different perspective from the other report:

> "The land which we passed through to spy out is an exceedingly good land. If the Lord is pleased with us, then He will bring us into this land and give it to us—a land which flows with milk and honey. Only do not rebel against the Lord; and do not fear the people of the land, for they will be our prey. Their protection is gone from them, and the Lord is with us; do not fear them." (Numbers 14:7-9)

Eight of the spies listened to their senses and lost complete perspective on the might and power of their God. Joshua and Caleb, like David, walked by faith and not by sight and were confident in God's power from past battles and victories and declared that fact boldly to their fellow Israelites:

> ".... go up and take possession of it, for we will
> certainly prevail over it" (Numbers 13:30)

We should also be cautioned here by the fact that not one of the eight spies who brought back negative information ever entered the Promised Land. They perished in the wilderness because of their unbelief:

> ".... the men who brought an evil report about
> the land, died by the pestilence before the LORD."
> (Numbers 14:36)

Like David, Joshua, and Caleb, we are called to use our faith and embrace the power and presence of God in our day-to-day lives.

We are exhorted not to be phased by life's situations and circumstances that can threaten to overwhelm us but to invest faith consistently in the eternal provision of God.

As Christian believers, we have the promise of Christ's victory to rely upon:

> "Now thanks be to God who always causes us to
> triumph in Christ and through us reveals the fra-
> grance of His knowledge in every place." (2 Corin-
> thians 2:14)

## CHAPTER NINETEEN

# What Is Sanctification?

In Chapter Eight, we investigated the significance of addressing God as, 'Abba Father' and we discovered that when we were 'born again', we were adopted into the family of God and, at the same time, He became our Heavenly Father.

Paul writes to that effect:

> "He predestined us to adoption as sons to Himself through Jesus Christ according to the good plea-sure of His will" (Ephesians 1:5)

One of the most significant features of being adopted is that one is selected and specially chosen and, in this case by God, Himself and what is more, it is 'to the good pleasure of His will'.

God takes special care in choosing us and is likewise, delighted to bring us into His Family.

The whole meaning of sanctification, therefore, is so much more understandable when you consider, that you have been sin-gled out, selected, and then placed lovingly into God's family.

When I was a young Christian, sanctification was a word that I never fully understood, and it was also a subject that ministers never seemed to explain.

The other problem seemed to be that the word itself, was slightly odd and not one that seemed to be used in everyday lan-guage. When you look for an initial definition of sanctification, it is that characteristic that is frequently highlighted - it is a relatively obscure word.

The word itself, first appeared in the fourteenth century, and was used almost exclusively, in a religious context and rarely appeared in a secular language.

Its religious usage though, is not just in a Christian context – it is used in other major religions as well.

However, in the Christian context, it appears in its various forms over one hundred and forty times in the Bible; thirty of those being in the New Testament.

If we look at the New Testament occurrences, we find that the word 'sanctification' is derived from the Greek words 'hagiasmos' meaning a state of purity or holiness, or "hagiazō" meaning 'to make holy or to ceremonially purify or consecrate'.

In the Old Testament, the process of sanctification was particularly evident in respect of the Tabernacle.

The Tabernacle was a temporary dwelling place where God could dwell among His people, the children of Israel, as they travelled through the desert.

What we see from the very moment that the construction of the tabernacle was completed, was that it had to be sanctified.

> "Moses took the anointing oil, and anointed the tabernacle and all that was in it and sanctified them".
> (Leviticus 8:10)

In other words, the Tabernacle and all the various items within it were carefully set apart and anointed with oil by Moses as a symbol of its holiness and dedication to God.

Everything was carefully selected; everything was sanctified and everything, had a specific God-ordained purpose.

Other examples in the Old Testament give us insights into this important process of sanctification.

As early as Genesis we see God, after Creation, setting apart and sanctifying the seventh day of the week:

> "And God blessed the seventh day and sanctified it: because that in it he had rested from all his work which God created and made". (Genesis 2:3)

So, we see that the seventh day was specifically selected by God and set apart for a clear purpose – a day to rest from work.

Jeremiah was told by God that he was sanctified to be a prophet even before he was born:

"Before I formed thee in the belly, I knew thee; and
before thou camest forth out of the womb I sanctified thee, and I ordained thee a prophet unto the
nations". (Jeremiah 1:5)

Jeremiah was carefully selected by God and set apart for a specific purpose – to be a prophet to the nations.

So, what does this process of sanctification have to do with us
as modern-day believers?

Does it apply to us and if so, how?

Peter writes to all believers:

"Elect according to the foreknowledge of God the
Father, through sanctification of the Spirit, unto
obedience and sprinkling of the blood of Jesus
Christ: Grace unto you, and peace, be multiplied"
(1 Peter 1:2)

We are much more than just saved, and we are more than just
members of the family of God.

Just like the Tabernacle, the Sabbath, and Jeremiah, we are also
specifically set apart through the sanctification of the Spirit for the
purpose and will of God.

Paul adds to Peter's revelation in his letter to the Thessalonians
and highlights the necessity of holiness and purification:

'For ye know what commandments we gave you
by the Lord Jesus. For this is the will of God, even
your sanctification, that ye should abstain from for-
nication: that every one of you should know how
to possess his vessel in sanctification and honour".
(1 Thessalonians 4:3-4)

Paul exhorts them to recognise that they are sanctified and set
apart for the purpose and will of God. He also emphasises that
they should understand how to maintain a state of spiritual purity
to ensure that the purpose of being 'set apart' is maintained in an
honourable state before God.

Paul relating his calling by God, to take the Gospel to the Gentiles says:

"To open their eyes, and to turn them from darkness to light, and from the power of Satan unto God, that they may receive forgiveness of sins, and inheritance among them which are sanctified by faith that is in me". (Acts 26:18)

Salvation here is to be seen as not only about a wonderful future inheritance but is again about being set apart or 'sanctified' for the purpose and will of God.

So, we as believers are not only saved but also sanctified.

The Tabernacle and every item in it needed to be sanctified because it was the dwelling place of God, so we too must be sanctified because we are members of the Church of Jesus Christ, the place where God presently dwells.

It's of vital importance that we grasp the importance of how our being sanctified impacts our individual lives.

Did you know you too were sanctified by God even before you were born?

"But You are He who took me out of the womb; you caused me to trust while I was on my mother's breasts." (Psalm 22:9)

Do you know the specific reason God has selected and sanctified you and set you apart?

Open your heart and mind to the Holy Spirit and allow him to reveal to you the reality and purpose of your sanctification.

"That the God of our Lord Jesus Christ, the Father of glory, may give unto you the spirit of wisdom and revelation in the knowledge of him: the eyes of your understanding being enlightened; that ye may know what the hope of his calling is, and what the riches of the glory of his inheritance in the saints". (Ephesians 1:17-18)

## CHAPTER TWENTY

# Work Out Your Own Salvation.

W e just looked at the meaning of sanctification and saw that our salvation needs to be seen as not only about a wonderful future inheritance in heaven but also about being set apart or 'sanctified' for the purpose and will of God here on earth.

Paul takes that process of sanctification much further when writing to the Philippian church.

He wants them to understand completely what it means not just to be saved, and sanctified, but also how our salvation and our sanctification are to be enacted in and through our lives.

He says:

> "Therefore, my beloved, as you have always obeyed,
> not only in my presence but so much more in my
> absence, work out your own salvation with fear and
> trembling." (Philippians 2:12)

This is an intriguing verse for all of us as believers because Paul seems to be highlighting a clear level of personal responsibility for overseeing and taking care of our salvation.

His exhortation is aimed at getting the Philippians to do something he felt was very important and needed to be carried out with a degree of seriousness and diligence.

The first part of his exhortation is to "work out."

Interestingly, this phrase is used in modern language and describes accurately what Paul had in mind.

"A workout" usually means some form of physical exercise to get you fit, keep you healthy, and provide you with a more active lifestyle.

Paul is encouraging the Philippians to think similarly about their salvation.

The Greek word he uses for 'work', is 'katergazomai' and it's helpful if we look at a far wider meaning of the Greek word for 'work' than the English translation would suggest.

'Katergazomai' means to work to bring something to fulfilment or successful completion and implies doing something with thoroughness.

The word also means to focus on those things that produce results and always means to complete the effort and the work begun.

Paul is directing them to take some responsibility here and put real energy and commitment into the overall development of what their salvation is and what it means.

To help our understanding, we also need to understand how Paul defines 'salvation'.

The Greek word he is using is 'sōtēria' meaning "the act of preserving or the state of being preserved from harm". Again, the word for 'salvation' has a much broader meaning in the original Greek than how we think of it in modern English.

Other meanings of the word 'sōtēria' include restoration to a state of safety, soundness, health, and well-being as well as preservation from the danger of destruction.

What Paul is saying here, defines our salvation as being far more than the 'one-off' experience of being born again when we embrace Christ as Saviour and join the family of God.

He positions our initial 'born-again' experience of salvation as a starting point of a journey.

Whilst the birth of a child is a wonderful thing and worthy of great celebration, it's also the beginning of a life that needs to progress, over time, to maturity.

Paul describes our salvation in the same way. It is the start of an important spiritual journey, over which we must take a level of personal responsibility by investing time, energy, and commitment.

Whilst the actual process of growing and progressing is enabled by the Holy Spirit, our role is to collaborate fully with Him and allow that maturing process to take place within our lives.

The value of investing our time and energy is not just about maintaining our spiritual well-being, it is also about making genuine progress on our journey toward spiritual maturity.

Paul describes the 'journey' this way:

> "Therefore, let us leave the elementary doctrine of Christ and go on to maturity, not laying again a foundation of repentance from dead works and of faith toward God" (Hebrews 6:1)

He adds to this description, by emphasising the destination of our journey in his letter to Ephesians:

> "Until we all attain to the unity of the faith and of the knowledge of the Son of God, to mature manhood, to the measure of the stature of the fullness of Christ." (Ephesians 4:13)

Paul completes our original verse by describing what our attitude and mindset should be concerning "working out our salvation."

He describes it as, "with fear and trembling."

This choice of words may, at first sight, be rather odd.

Fear? Trembling?

They are words that one usually associates with something you need help to overcome!

Once again, we need to understand the actual meaning of the words that Paul chooses to use.

The Greek word Paul uses for fear is "phobos", meaning actual human fear or "deep respect", which is the meaning that Paul is applying here.

The Greek word for "trembling" is "tromos" which has a very interesting meaning.

'Tromos' can be used to describe the anxiety of one who distrusts his ability completely to meet the given requirements, but religiously does his utmost to fulfil his duty.

So, what does that mean?

Paul is deliberately using the phrase "fear and trembling" to clarify precisely what our attitude and mindset should be here and not leave any room for misunderstanding.

He is saying that we should 'work out our salvation' by approaching our journey toward spiritual maturity with every ounce of human energy, commitment, and diligence we can muster.

We should do so, in the full knowledge, that we must never trust that personal energy and commitment to be enough on their own.

However, that totality of human commitment is, nonetheless, still vitally important.

That totality of our commitment and compliance is the ultimate requirement that the Holy Spirit requires from each of us.

This totality of commitment and compliance, that proverbial one hundred percent, is what Paul describes, as our "reasonable service":

> "I beseech you therefore, brethren, by the mercies of God, that ye present your bodies a living sacrifice, holy, acceptable unto God, which is your reasonable service." (Romans 12:1)

We will always need the guidance, strength, and support of the Holy Spirit, to take us successfully toward the goal of maturity and to the ultimate approval of God.

However, Christ also requires us to give everything we have and everything we possess, to bring us to that position of spiritual maturity and God's ultimate approval.

If we comply and collaborate with the Holy Spirit, then we have that assurance that Paul goes on to describe in his letter to the Philippian church:

> "I am confident of this very thing, that He who began a good work in you will perfect it until the day of Jesus Christ" (Philippians 1:6)

## CHAPTER TWENTY-ONE

# Be Approved!

We have just seen how Paul exhorted the church in Philippi to 'work out their own salvation with fear and trembling'.

Paul, writing to the young minister, Timothy also encourages him to be diligent and committed to his spiritual life and his ministerial calling.

This piece of encouragement which we will look at briefly is a good example of two principles we have already covered.

One principle is the purpose of sanctification and of Timothy being set apart for the service of Christ.

The other is the principle we have just looked at - investing energy and commitment in our spiritual journey with Him.

So, to what end is Paul encouraging Timothy?

In the original translation into English, the King James Version, this encouragement is translated as:

> "Study to shew thyself approved unto God, a workman that needeth not to be ashamed, rightly dividing the word of truth." (2 Timothy 2:15)

Paul is indicating to Timothy that there is a definite end point to this process of 'studying' and it is to be eventually approved by God as a mature and trusted minister of His Word.

However, we need to take a look at the word 'study' because it is frequently used by ministers to be almost exclusively to do with studying the Scriptures.

That connection is usually based on the conventional sense of studying being a very book-based activity.

The actual meaning of the verse is however quite different from the traditional understanding of many Christians.

From the outset, we can see that in the text there is no mention of the Scriptures. Some might say that "the word of truth" used by Paul infers the Scriptures or the Bible as we know it, but that is not stated or indicated by him in either verse.

As we will see, the deeper and true meaning of the verse is far more impactful.

Again, that deeper meaning is hidden within the original Greek word for "study," which had a far different application in Paul's era than how we use it today.

Our current usage of the word "study" originated from the Latin and French words "occupatur" and "estudiier" respectively.

Interestingly, this stronger connection, between 'books' and 'study', doesn't appear in any European language until at least the 1300s.

The noun, 'a study', meaning a room reserved for studying and usually depicted with a desk and shelves full of books, also appears around the same time.

However, we do know the Scriptures play an important part in Paul's encouragement to Timothy because he also refers him to the holy Scriptures as:

> "Making you wise unto salvation…." (2 Timothy 3:15).

"Study," though as it is originally used by Paul, is the Greek word 'spoudazo' and it means 'to make effort, to be diligent and to labour'.

If you apply those meanings to his exhortation to Timothy, then you get a different kind of emphasis than simply studying conventionally.

Paul is exhorting and encouraging Timothy to see himself as sanctified and set apart for the work of God.

This is the real purpose of Paul's encouragement of Timothy.

He is exhorting him to apply himself diligently and enthusiastically to his Christian faith and be fully committed to his heavenly calling as a true disciple and minister of Christ.

Paul concludes with another exhortation to Timothy, which also reaches down through time and includes each one of us:

> "Giving no offence in anything, that the ministry
> be not blamed: but in all things approving ourselves

as the ministers of God, in much patience, in afflictions, in necessities, in distresses, in stripes, in imprisonments, in tumults, in labours, in watchings, in fastings; by pureness, by knowledge, by longsuffering, by kindness, by the Holy Ghost, by love unfeigned". (2 Timothy 6:3-6)

# CHAPTER TWENTY-TWO

# 'Be Transformed'

In the previous chapter, we investigated what Paul meant when he spoke about 'working out our salvation with fear and trembling.'

We saw our salvation was not just a 'one-off' event of being born again, but also the start of an important spiritual journey towards spiritual maturity.

It is a journey of complete collaboration with the Holy Spirit.

It is a journey, where we are exhorted to walk by faith and invest time, energy, and commitment to make progress towards maturity.

Whilst the actual process of maturing spiritually is enabled by the Holy Spirit, we have seen that it is our responsibility to collaborate fully with Him to allow that process to take place within our lives.

In this chapter, we are going to take a closer look at how that process of maturing takes place.

Paul writing to the Roman church said this:

> "Do not be conformed to this world, but be transformed by the renewing of your mind, that you may prove what is the good and acceptable and perfect will of God" (Romans 12:2)

This verse is remarkable, containing powerful insights into the nature of our journey with Christ.

There are several different, yet connected, elements to Paul's instructional message to the Roman church.

The first element that he highlights is "Do not be conformed to this world...."

Paul, from the start, is firmly emphasising what their stance and approach needs to be concerning the worldly environment in which they lived their normal lives.

The Greek word he uses for 'conform' is 'suschēmatizō' which means to form or mould one's behaviour following a particular pattern or set of earthly standards.

His exhortation is very clear that they should never attempt to shape or configure their earthly lives to align with the transient fashions and passing customs of this world.

Paul also highlighted this principle in his letter to the Colossians:

> "If then you have been raised with Christ, seek the things that are above, where Christ is, seated at the right hand of God. Set your minds on things that are above, not on things that are on earth." (Colossians 3:1-2)

John echoes Paul's words:

> "Do not love the world or the things in the world. If anyone loves the world, the love of the Father is not in him. For all that is in the world—the lust of the flesh, the lust of the eyes, and the pride of life—is not of the Father but is of the world. The world and its desires are passing away, but the one who does the will of God lives forever" (1 John 2:15-17)

Paul then moves on from what we should refrain from, and emphasises what it is, that we should focus upon:

> ".... but be transformed by the renewing of your mind......"

The Greek word for 'transform' is 'metaschēmatizo', and it means to remodel, restructure or mutate the form of a person or thing.

The English word 'metamorphosis' is derived from the same word.

Its meaning is quite significant in terms of what Paul is highlighting in this verse.

The word means 'a marked change in appearance, character, condition or function.'

What Paul is emphasising here, is a most important part of our Christian walk, and it is concerned with the Holy Spirit, remodelling, and changing us, from within.

This is the process of becoming mature that we looked at in the previous chapter.

As human beings, we grow up and, in the process, we are shaped and literally, transformed into mature adults from those things we experience and learn from life.

When we are born again, we enter the family of God but like a new-born baby, we also need to grow and mature.

Similarly, Paul is exhorting us to allow the Holy Spirit to enact that same process of maturing and subsequent transformation to take place in our spiritual lives.

Growing up and maturing spiritually is synonymous with the process of being transformed, step by step.

He describes that growing and transforming process in his letter to the Ephesians:

> "Rather, speaking the truth in love, we are to grow up in every way into him who is the head, into Christ" (Ephesians 4:15)

So, what is clearer now is that this transformation process, enabled by the Holy Spirit, causes us to become increasingly Christ-like over time.

Whilst Paul encourages the Roman church, by contrast, he scolds the Corinthian church for remaining worldly, and not progressing and maturing into spiritual adulthood:

> "Brothers, I could not speak to you as to spiritual men, but as to worldly, even as to babes in Christ. I have fed you with milk and not with solid food. For to this day, you were not able to endure it. Nor are you able now, for you are still worldly" (1 Corinthians 3:1-3).

Paul then moves to the next important element of our verse:

> "....be transformed by the renewing of your mind......"

Paul declares that the process of spiritual transformation is enabled by "the renewing of your mind".

The Greek word here for 'renewing' is 'anakainósis' which means a renewal or change of heart and life, a literal makeover of the mind and soul.

It also means to move from one stage to a higher stage.

So, let us be clear that spiritual renewal is not a process of self-improvement that we enact ourselves.

The current, secular world is full of self-improvement processes and literature that have no place in the Body of Christ.

In the Body of Christ, we have but one self-improvement process, and that is the one enacted completely, by the Holy Spirit.

Whilst this renewal process must be collaborative, the actual renewing itself is exclusively and solely the work of the Holy Spirit.

Paul is, therefore, exhorting the Roman church to allow the Holy Spirit to work in them spiritually so that this transformation into the image of Christ can take place.

Paul put it this way when writing to the Galatians:

> "My little children, of whom I labour in birth again
> until Christ is formed in you" (Galatians 4:19).

The Greek word for "formed" is "morpho."

The English word "morph" is derived from the same word.

"Morph" means to gradually change or change someone or something from one thing to another.

That is precisely what the work of the Holy Spirit is – shaping and forming us, from within, into the image of Christ.

Paul then moves to the final piece of our verse by clarifying the ultimate purpose of this step-by-step transformation by the Holy Spirit.

> "…. that you may prove what is the good and
> acceptable and perfect will of God"

The Greek word for 'prove' is "dokimazo" which means to 'test' or 'examine'.

Paul is stressing here that the Holy Spirit wants them to mature and be transformed spiritually, so that they can know and assess more precisely what the perfect will and purpose of God is, at every step of their spiritual journey.

He specifically states what this ability to 'test and examine' means when, like the Corinthians, Paul rebukes the Hebrew church for being babies and not progressing toward maturity:

> "For though by now you should be teachers, you need someone to teach you again the first principles of the oracles of God and have come to need milk rather than solid food."

> "Everyone who lives on milk is unskilled in the word of righteousness, for he is a baby. But solid food belongs to those who are mature, for those who through practice have powers of discernment that are trained to distinguish good from evil." (Hebrews 5:12-14)

He shows his extreme concern for them as their immaturity means they are spiritually vulnerable because they have had no experience developing their spiritual judgment, to skilfully distinguish between what is good and what is evil.

Jesus was, for thirty years, growing and maturing; being prepared to carry out the perfect will of His Father.

Even in his youth, we see this growing and maturing taking place:

> "And Jesus increased in wisdom and stature and favour with God and men. (Acts 2:52)

He declared:

> "My food is to do the will of Him who sent Me, and to finish His work." (John 4:34)

Jesus needed to become mature and be made ready and then be approved by His Father before commencing His earthly ministry.

His Father endorsed him as He came out of the water at John's baptism:

> "And a voice came from heaven, saying, "You are My beloved Son in whom I am well pleased" (Mark 1:11)

So, the process of maturing is about allowing the Holy Spirit to progressively transform us on our journey toward maturity.

It is a journey where we obediently and consistently acquiesce to the Holy Spirit, so that:

> "We may grow up in all things into Him, who is the Head, Christ Himself" (Ephesians 4:15)

## CHAPTER TWENTY-THREE

# 'Demas Has Left Me'

"Therefore, since we are encompassed with such a great cloud of witnesses, let us also lay aside every weight and the sin that so easily entangles us, and let us run with endurance the race that is set before us." (Hebrews 12:1).

Here, in his letter to the Hebrew church, Paul describes our spiritual journey as a spiritual race and compares us to athletes.

Notice that he again stresses the need to turn away from any worldly activities and unnecessary concerns, which will distract and divert us away from 'the race' that God has set before us.

He also uses the word 'endurance' to describe how we should approach this spiritual race.

He is suggesting that this race is certainly not a short sprint but much more of a distance event.

He is also stressing that we should be determined to get to the winning post and reach for the prize.

> "Do you not know that all those who run in a race run, but one receives the prize? So run, that you may obtain it. (1 Corinthians 9:24)

However, not everybody who runs the race completes the course.

Not everybody that starts the journey, completes the journey.

Jesus warned his disciples, about the consequences of turning back from the path, which God has laid out for us:

> "No one who puts his hand to the plough and looks back at things is fit for the kingdom of God." (Luke 9:62)

Demas is an example of someone who started well but then turned back.

There are very few scriptural references to Demas, so we have very little information with which to work.

We know that he accompanied Paul on his travels, and he is included in Paul's greeting to the church at Colossae:

> "Luke, the beloved physician, and Demas greet you." (Colossians 4:14)

He is also mentioned by Paul again in his very short letter to Philemon:

> "Epaphras, my fellow prisoner in Christ Jesus, greets you, as do Mark, Aristarchus, Demas, and Luke, my fellow labourers" (Philemon 1:23-24)

The only other reference to Demas is in Paul's second letter to Timothy:

> "Demas has forsaken me, having loved this present world, and has departed to Thessalonica…" (2 Timothy 4:10)

So, with limited information, we can only speculate as to what had occurred to cause Demas to abandon Paul, his ministry, and his Christian faith.

Paul is not specific about precisely what circumstances had occurred to cause Demas to take this action, but we do know that some worldly seduction has taken place which he found extremely appealing.

Paul's words are very clear:

> "Demas…. having loved this present world…."

The Greek word for 'love', here, is 'agapaō' which would infer Demas had a 'strong affection' or 'deep fondness' for whatever worldly attractions seduced him away from Christ, from Paul, and his ministry.

Paul also describes the way Demas left him.

The Greek word for 'forsaken' is 'egkataleipō' which means 'to desert,' 'to leave helpless', or to 'totally abandon'.

This Greek verb implies that Demas had not merely left Paul but had left him 'in the lurch;' that is, Demas had abandoned Paul in a time of need.

'Egkataleipō' is the same word in Greek, that Jesus used when dying on the cross:

> "About the ninth hour, Jesus cried out with a loud voice, "Eli, Eli, lama sabachthani?" which means, "My God, My God, why have You forsaken Me" (Matthew 27:46)

So here was Paul, in a crisis himself, in prison, facing a death sentence, and that is precisely when Demas chose to abandon him.

Undoubtedly, Paul was deeply let down by Demas.

One other thing we do know is, that when he left Paul, Demas went to Thessalonica.

Thessalonica was a major city of the Roman Republic. It had grown to be an important trade hub, which facilitated trade between Europe and Asia.

We must think that a city of this size and importance would also be home to every conceivable worldly attraction one can imagine.

Paul's own experience of this city was also a turbulent one.

Although he had established a Christian church there, he had also made archenemies of certain violent members of the Jewish community because of preaching Christ as the Messiah:

> "Some of the Jews were persuaded and joined Paul and Silas, as did a large number of God-fearing Greeks and quite a few prominent women. But other Jews were jealous; so, they rounded up some bad characters from the marketplace, formed a mob, and started a riot in the city. They rushed to Jason's house in search of Paul and Silas in order to bring them out to the crowd" (Acts 17:4-5)

So did Demas choose Thessalonica because, as a major Roman city, it offered every worldly attraction one could imagine?

Or was he financially induced to become a propaganda figure for those Jewish activists who were violently opposed to Paul and his Christian message?

Was Demas' betrayal of Paul, in fact, very similar to Judas Iscariot's betrayal of Jesus?

We cannot be sure, but one thing we can be sure of is also a warning to us all:

> "Do not love the world or the things in the world.
> If anyone loves the world, the love of the Father is
> not in him." (1 John 2:15)

## CHAPTER TWENTY-FOUR

# Growing and Maturing in Christ

One of the most disappointing aspects of my business career as an independent marketing and sales consultant was the apparent disinterest among many adults in the process of continuous learning and professional growth.

The words 'developing' and 'growing' here relate to an individual's overall development as a responsible and mature adult with the ability to make a personal and valuable contribution in some recognisable way.

For many, it seemed that the whole need to learn, grow, and develop oneself ceased almost completely at the point of leaving school or college.

It is sad to say that, in my experience, a similar mindset seems to also exist across a lot of the Christian Church.

The whole concept of growing up and maturing spiritually seems to be yet another area of teaching that has been sadly neglected, as we have seen already.

The Scriptures, though have many, very clear references to the need to grow up and mature as Christian believers.

Our primary example, as always, must be Jesus.

Luke particularly is very clear about Jesus' spiritual growth and progress toward maturity:

> "And the Child grew and became strong in spirit,
> filled with wisdom; and the grace of God was upon
> Him" (Luke 2:40)

Even though he was the Son of God, he also needed to take responsibility for his humanity and its challenges as the Son of Man.

This meant embracing the rigours of learning, growing, and progressing towards becoming a mature man.

Paul adds to our understanding of Jesus' growth and maturing:

> ".... though He was a Son, yet He learned obedience by the things which He suffered. And having been perfected, He became the author of eternal salvation to all who obey Him".

We can see here that there was a clear purpose to this overall maturing process which was to be the perfect and complete Saviour of us all.

The exhortation then, is for us as believers to grow and mature like Christ grew and matured.

Peter tells us to:

> "Grow in the grace and knowledge of our Lord and Saviour Jesus Christ" (2 Peter 3:18).

He indicates clearly that knowing Jesus is the most significant part of the maturing process.

Notice he says, "grow in grace' and not just simply acquire 'knowledge' about Jesus. Gaining knowledge about Jesus is one thing, but increasing our spiritual insight of who He is, is something quite different.

Peter goes on to emphasise, as we saw Paul emphasising earlier, that we should lay aside everything that could distract us and focus on 'the milk of the word' to grow and mature as believers:

He says:

> "Therefore, laying aside all malice, all deceit, hypocrisy, envy, and all evil speaking, as new-born babes, desire the pure milk of the word, that you may grow thereby" (1 Peter 1-2).

The focus here again is not simply hearing the living Word and understanding it, but on 'growing.'

Notice though that Peter here is referring to 'new-born babes' and what is needed to start the process of spiritual growth- 'the pure milk of the word.'

However, Paul goes on to emphasise that 'the milk of the word' was never intended to be a permanent diet for believers.

He stresses that we should look to move on from milk to solid food as soon as possible.

He says to the Hebrews:

> "For though by this time you ought to be teach-
> ers, you need someone to teach you again the first
> principles of the oracles of God, and you have
> come to need milk and not solid food. For every-
> one who partakes only of milk is unskilled in the
> word of righteousness, for he is a babe". (Ephe-
> sians 5:12-13).

Notice Paul's point here, he is stating that they should be teach-
ers of others by now and have become important contributors to
the Body of Christ, but they have not grown up and matured and
still want milk as opposed to solid food. He scolds them because
they still need to be taught and fed by others, just like babies. They
are still 'takers' and not 'givers'!

He states a very similar truth to the church at Corinth:

> "And I, brethren, could not speak to you as to spir-
> itual people but as to carnal, as to babes in Christ. I
> fed you with milk and not with solid food; for until
> now you were not able to receive it, and even now
> you are still not able" (1 Corinthians 3:1-2)

We all know that children must grow out of a diet of milk and
their total reliance on their mothers.

Similarly, believers also need to grow up and grow out of the
need to be reliant on others to administer their spiritual food when
they should be feeding fellow believers.

Part of the problem lies in the fact that many of our churches
have been led primarily by one person, who ministers to the same
congregation, week in and week out.

Christians, fellowshipping in that environment will always
become very dependent on others to feed them, they will never
develop the sense of responsibility or the capacity to feed themselves and feed others.

What's so distressing is, that we know that this whole

responsibility to care and share with our fellow believers and to minister to each other, is at the heart of what the Body of Christ is all about.

Jesus warned of the consequences of this over-reliance on others in the parable of the wise and foolish virgins:

> "Then all those virgins rose and trimmed their lamps. But the foolish said to the wise, 'Give us some of your oil, for our lamps have gone out. The wise answered, 'No, lest there not be enough for us and you. Go rather to those who sell it and buy some for yourselves." (Matthew 25:7-9)

Paul takes the whole issue of growing and maturing and describes it in far more important terms, he exhorts us to be less and less like spiritual infants, relying heavily on others for nourishment and he encourages us to become more adult and more mature. He stresses that we should be increasingly Christ-like in our daily lives and in our overall capacity to contribute to the Body of Christ:

He puts it this way:

> "…. that we should no longer be children, tossed to and fro and carried about with every wind of doctrine, by the trickery of men, in the cunning craftiness of deceitful plotting, but, speaking the truth in love, may grow up in all things into Him who is the head—Christ" (Ephesians 4:14-15).

The complete purpose of the Body of Christ is that we feed each other as we are also fed by the Holy Spirit for this is the way the Body of Christ grows together, and how we progressively become more and more Christ-like.

Paul puts it simply:

> "How is it then, brethren? Whenever you come together, each of you has a psalm, has a teaching, has a tongue, has a revelation, has an interpretation. Let all things be done for edification" (1 Corinthians 14:26)

The key word here is "edification" meaning, we build each other up and provide each member with the nourishment, with which to grow. It means we not only need to grow ourselves, but we also share an equal responsibility for contributing to the spiritual growth of the whole Body of Christ and to each member.

And to what end?

What is the real purpose of God here?

Paul states it clearly:

> "So (we) may grow up in all things into Him who is the head—Christ, from whom the whole body, joined and knit together by what every joint supplies, according to the effective working by which every part does its share, causes growth of the body for the edifying of itself in love" (Ephesians 4:15-16)

CHAPTER TWENTY-FIVE

# The Power of Prayer

We have so far, stressed the absolute need for active faith to underpin our walk with Christ.

We know that:

> "Without faith, it's impossible to please God".
> (Hebrews 11:6)

We also know that:

> "We walk by faith and not by sight". (2 Corinthians 5:7)

However, given this level of importance in our lives, how do we maintain a strong level of faith?

One way is by using our faith constantly and consistently and by applying the promises of God in every aspect of our lives.

It's a simple principle, that what you use or apply regularly, will also become stronger with use and will become the increasingly natural way you walk with Christ.

There is though one other important principle to which we need to pay attention.

Paul emphasises this principle in his second letter to Timothy:

> "For these things I suffer, but I am not ashamed, for I know whom I have believed, and am persuaded that He is able to keep that which I have committed to Him until that Day." (2 Timothy 1:12-14)

The principle is revealed in the words, "I know whom I have believed and am persuaded that He is able...."

His point is very simple to understand because it is something most of us have experienced in our daily lives.

The more you know someone, the more you are likely to trust them.

The more you trust them, the more you are likely to believe what they tell you.

It is also true, that the more we know Christ, the more likely we are to hear His voice.

It is at this point that we need to understand and embrace the power of prayer because it is a most important part of our journey of faith and our walk with Christ.

James reassures us:

"Draw near to God, and He will draw near to you"
(James 4:8)

Whether we pray as part of our communion with the Lord or as an intercession for others, we should see it as an ever-increasingly active part of our daily lives.

Paul stresses the function of prayer when writing to the church in Thessalonica:

"Pray without ceasing" (1 Thessalonians 5:17)

He is stressing the need for us to see prayer as a continuous and consistent part of our spiritual lives.

He positions prayer, as much an integral part of our spiritual well-being, as breathing fresh air is to our human life.

He expands further on both the importance of prayer and what the focus of our prayers should be when writing to the church in Ephesus:

".... praying at all times in the Spirit, with all prayer and supplication. To that end, keep alert with all perseverance, making supplication for all the saints" (Ephesians 6:18)

Jesus' life was the ultimate example.

His life was constantly punctuated with specific and quality prayer time with his Father.

He saw the absolute need to find the time and an appropriate location to commune, pray, and stay intimately close to his Father.

The Gospels give us clear examples of how and where he took that time to pray.

> "One day soon afterward he went out into the mountains to pray and prayed all night." (Luke 6:12).

> "And when he had sent the multitudes away, he went up into a mountain apart to pray and when the evening came, he was there alone" (Matthew 14:23)

He saw prayer as incredibly important,

He saw it as so important that he gave his disciples very clear instructions about how to pray:

"And when you pray, you must not be like the hypocrites. For they love to stand and pray in the synagogues and at the street corners, so that they may be seen by others.

> "Truly, I say to you, they have received their reward. But when you pray, go into your room, and shut the door and pray to your Father who is in secret. And your Father who sees in secret will reward you. And when you pray, do not heap up empty phrases as the Gentiles do, for they think that they will be heard for their many words. Do not be like them, for your Father knows what you need before you ask him" (Matthew 6:5-8)

He also gave them important guidance on what to pray for. Mark recalls one such piece of guidance:

> "And when you stand praying, forgive if you have anything against anyone, so that your Father who is in heaven may also forgive you your sins" (Mark 11:25)

Matthew provides another example; this time of who to pray for:

> "But I say to you, love your enemies and pray for those who persecute you" (Matthew 5:44)

In the Early Church, they engaged in prayer together, before they were filled with the Holy Spirit on the Day of Pentecost and consistently afterward.

As directed by Jesus, they gathered in Jerusalem to await the arrival of the Holy Spirit and prayer was a key part of how they spent that time together, waiting:

> "These all continued with one accord in prayer and supplication, with the women, and Mary the mother of Jesus, and with his brethren" (Acts 1:14)

After Pentecost, we still see prayer as an integral part of the apostles' daily lives:

> "Brothers, look among yourselves for seven men who are known to be full of the Holy Spirit and wisdom, whom we will appoint over this duty. But we will give ourselves continually to prayer and the ministry of the word." (Acts 6:3-4)

His exhortation to the church in Philippi was probably an exhortation that he had almost certainly expressed elsewhere:

> "Do not be anxious about anything, but in every-thing by prayer and supplication with thanksgiving let your requests be made known to God. And the peace of God, which surpasses all understanding, will guard your hearts and your minds in Christ Jesus" (Philippians 4:6-7)

On a personal level, the more we find quality time for prayer and fellowship with the Father, the more our relationship with Him will develop and mature, the more our relationship with Him matures through prayer, the more we will hear His voice and the more we will learn to have faith in His Word and in His promises.

Paul points directly to the connection between hearing His voice and the subsequent stimulation of our faith:

> "So then faith comes by hearing, and hearing by the word of God." (Romans 10:17)

As a result, our lives will increasingly become a clearer reflection of His nature and character.

Our more focused prayer life will mean that we become more consciously led and directed by the Holy Spirit.

On a collective level, prayer together should also become much more the norm. We are exhorted to bear one another's burdens, intercede for those in personal need, and to hold each other up before the Lord.

Praying and interceding for each other is one of the clearest examples of Christ's love in action.

Let us boldly pay heed to Paul's words:

> "And take the helmet of salvation, and the sword of the Spirit, which is the word of God: Praying always with all prayer and supplication in the Spirit and watching thereunto with all perseverance and supplication for all saints" (Ephesians 6:17-18).

## CHAPTER TWENTY-SIX

# The Value of Fellowship

I seem to be having more and more conversations with fellow Christians about where, how, and when to extend their fellowship with other believers. There is an increasing and noticeable hunger among many believers to find ways to build new and extended connections with other believers.

A common theme is the desire to build bridges with those who share a genuine commitment to the complete Gospel of Jesus, and one which is aligned with the example and foundational practices and principles of the early Church.

In many situations, this has come about from either a genuine dissatisfaction with their existing church or more frequently, a desire to move on with Christ in a new and more mature way.

I do not believe that these desires are in any way, a coincidence. They reflect how the Holy Spirit is drawing "those who hunger and thirst after righteousness" into a more extended fellowship. Fellowship, where they can "be filled" via the contribution of other members of the Body of Christ, who are attuned to the moving of the Holy Spirit.

During the time, of what was commonly known as "Charismatic Renewal" in the 60s and 70s, there were many who were not sure of whether they should stay in their current church or leave. I do not think there was an easy answer then and there isn't today.

The leading of the Holy Spirit is the only way forward, you should always take your lead from that one, utterly reliable source.

However, whether you are meant to stay or leave, increasing and extending your circle of fellowship, either locally or remotely, is something you should enquire about with the Lord. I say 'remote' because, during Covid, many of us relied much more on technology to maintain fellowship, when we were more isolated. Technology is a widely available tool, and we should try to use it to reach out to other believers, either by simple messaging or via video links.

God is preparing His people in the last days.

We should not neglect fellowship with like-minded believers as the functioning Body of Christ is the Holy Spirit's way of speaking directly to us, affirming His Will, teaching us, and providing us with important direction.

Paul said quite deliberately:

> "Not forsaking the assembling of ourselves together, as the manner of some is but exhorting one another: and so much the more, as ye see the day approaching". (Hebrews in 10:25)

See how he pinpoints the importance of fellowship.

What should I do about fellowship? He exhorts that we do not forsake it.

For what purpose? To optimise fellowship with fellow believers, for mutual sharing, ministry, and edification. Why? Because the day of the Lord approaches. Jesus is returning soon.

The way of the flesh and carnal thinking, aided and abetted by Satan, is to separate, divide, and cause disunity in the Church, which we see so evidenced, currently.

Paul, warning the Corinthian church, says:

> "For while one says, "I am of Paul," and another, "I am of Apollos," are you not worldly? (1 Corinthians 3:4)

I need you and you need me to grow in Christ. This need of each other should always be the common focus of our fellowship, as we seek out new connections, with new brothers and sisters in Christ:

> "How is it then, brethren? When ye come together, every one of you hath a psalm, hath a doctrine, hath a tongue, hath a revelation, hath an interpretation. Let all things be done unto edifying".

We absolutely need each other, and it is also God's way whereby we demonstrate the love of Christ to each other, it is also one of the important ways by which we grow and mature.

This is the true purpose of the Body of Christ:

> "From whom the whole body fitly joined together and compacted by that which every joint supplieth, according to the effectual working in the measure of every part, maketh increase of the body unto the edifying of itself in love." (Ephesians 4:16)

## CHAPTER TWENTY-SEVEN

# Communion

A while ago, I asked the Holy Spirit to give me a deeper sense of the role and meaning of what we know as Communion.

I have celebrated Communion for many years, and always seen it as an important part of a Sunday morning worship service. I had always done my very best to respect that part of the service, I tried to make sure that I acknowledged its meaning and purpose, as much as I knew and understood it.

So, for a considerable period of my life, I had embraced the importance of Communion to the Christian faith.

However, I slowly began to realise that I did not have a full sense of its true meaning and importance.

One of the very first things I uncovered on my voyage of discovery, was that Paul in his letter to the Corinthians had repeated almost word for word what Jesus had said to his disciples when he initiated the very first Communion at what we know, as the Last Supper.

Here is what Jesus said in Luke 22:18-20:

> "And He took bread, gave thanks and broke it, and gave it to them, saying, "This is My body which is given for you; do this in remembrance of Me." Likewise, He also took the cup after supper, saying, "This cup is the new covenant in My blood, which is shed for you."

Paul repeats Jesus' words in 1 Corinthians 11:25 and adds "… this do ye, as oft as ye drink it, in remembrance of me".

What I saw as important, immediately, was, that this is the only instance when Paul, in all his letters, repeating virtually word for word, an important statement made by Jesus, somebody, he never met physically.

This unique repetition by Paul is significant and places an unprecedented level of importance on the words of Jesus and the purpose of Communion itself.

It strongly suggests that when we fellowship together, we should also look to break the bread and drink the wine and do so with greater regularity.

We should allow the Holy Spirit to bring to the forefront of our minds the words of Jesus and, most importantly, what the bread and the wine both signify.

Many of those I fellowship with, have reported an increased desire to celebrate Communion more frequently, than just the traditional Sunday morning, each week.

This increased frequency seems to be related to a clearer understanding of what Paul meant when he wrote:

"…. as oft as you do this".

This growing desire to place more priority on Communion seems to be far more than simply a new Christian trend. It also seems to be something the Holy Spirit is stimulating us to do.

I believe a key reason for this sense of renewed priority is, that the blood of Christ and the Body of Christ, are truly at the heart of everything our salvation is based upon.

In the current climate, when the Christian truth is under unprecedented attack, from both the outside world and from within the Church, and the Gospel has been seriously reduced in its true potency, the Holy Spirit is, I believe, raising the importance of Communion, as a kind of 'red alert' to all believers, everywhere.

The Holy Spirit is admonishing us to not lose our focus, for one moment, on the foundation principles of our faith, which is what Communion affirms.

The bread and the wine represent that which redeems us, and also that which sustains us, as born-again believers.

Firstly, it affirms the Blood of Christ by which we are all completely redeemed and fully justified:

"In Him, we have redemption through His blood,
the forgiveness of sins, according to the riches of
His grace" (Ephesians 1:7)

It also affirms the Body of Christ by which we are nourished:

> "Jesus said to them, "I am the bread of life. Whoever comes to Me shall never hunger, and whoever believes in Me shall never thirst." (John 6:35)

We are sustained by Jesus, who is both the 'Bread of Life' and the 'Word made Flesh'.

So, what should we do?

Let us keep the Body and Blood of Christ at the forefront of everything we do as Christian believers. To maintain that perspective, we should take Communion, whenever we gather together for fellowship at any time, in any location.

Let us recognise that the elevating of the importance of Communion is something the Holy Spirit is doing and that also makes it an issue of obedience.

Above all, let us focus on the core meaning and purpose of Communion.

> "The cup of blessing which we bless, is it not the communion of the blood of Christ? The bread which we break, is it not the communion of the body of Christ? For we, though many, are one bread and one body; for we all partake of that one bread" (1 Corinthians 10:16-17)

## CHAPTER TWENTY-EIGHT

# Be a Berean – Test Everything!

T he Bereans, lived in the Greek city of Berea, also called Bercea, in the time of the Apostle Paul, about AD 50.

Berea has existed since around 400 BC and there are some indications that people lived in the area as early as 1000 BC. In the time of the Apostle Paul, it was part of the Roman Empire. Berea was originally in southwestern Macedonia but is now known as Veria and is located in northern Greece.

The Bereans are the people who are highlighted in Acts Seventeen and are most likely known, for searching and studying the Scriptures for themselves and not merely accepting what they were taught by Paul.

He acknowledged them to be "of more noble character" than those who simply listened but did not study the Scriptures carefully for themselves and test the authenticity of what they were hearing.

Paul clarifies:

> "These were more noble than those in Thessalonica, for they received the word with all eagerness, daily examining the Scriptures, to find out if these things were so." (Acts 17:11).

More interesting, is the fact that not only did they listen and conduct further research into what they were hearing, but it led many of them to believe in Jesus as their Messiah:

> "Therefore, many of them believed, including honourable Greek women and many Greek men." (Acts 17:12)

Notice that those who came to Christ were not just limited to the Jews within the synagogue, but also extended to many Greek men and women in Berea.

It's worth noting that Berea was also recognised, at the time, as a centre of Greek culture and learning, so we see that the Gospel was already gaining traction at some learned and cultural levels of Berean society.

The Bereans also took care of Paul's safety, when his enemies arrived from nearby Thessalonica.

The Berean believers protected Paul by transporting him out of the region:

> "But when the Jews of Thessalonica learned that the word of God was preached by Paul at Berea, they came there also, stirring up the crowds. The brothers immediately sent Paul away to the sea. But Silas and Timothy remained there" (Acts 17:13-14)

When Paul decided to return for additional ministry in Macedonia, one of the men who chose to accompany him was a Berean:

> "There he spent three months, and when a plot was made against him by the Jews as he was about to set sail for Syria, he decided to return through Macedonia. Sopater the Berean, son of Pyrrhus, accompanied him" (Acts 20:3-4).

So, where are the noble Bereans today?

Where are the Christian believers who will listen enthusiastically to God's Word but will also do their homework and research the accuracy and truthfulness of what they are hearing?

There are potential consequences if we blindly absorb teaching without checking its validity and source.

Let us heed to the words of Paul and be like the noble Bereans:

> "Prove all things; hold fast that which is good" (1 Thessalonians 5:21)

## CHAPTER TWENTY-NINE

# The Voice of the Holy Spirit

J esus was very clear:

> "My sheep hear My voice, and I know them, and
> they follow Me. I give them eternal life. They shall
> never perish, nor shall anyone snatch them from
> My hand." (John 10:27-28)

As we saw earlier, hearing His voice is an essential part of our Christian life and without it, we will most certainly lack spiritual direction and suffer from spiritual malnutrition.

As Jesus said:

> "It is written, 'Man shall not live by bread alone,
> but by every word that proceeds out of the mouth
> of God." (Matthew 4:4).

Hearing the voice of the Holy Spirit is of paramount importance to our spiritual well-being and health.

In the Old Testament, God spoke directly to selected individuals like Abraham, Moses, Samuel, and other noteworthy prophets like Isaiah, Jeremiah, and Daniel.

They became designated channels through whom, God spoke and gave direction, primarily to His chosen people, the Israelites.

Then Jesus arrived and:

> "The Word became flesh and dwelt among us, and
> we saw His glory, the glory as the only Son of the
> Father, full of grace and truth." (John 1:14)

Jesus ministered and taught the Israelites in person and so He was seen and experienced as that 'Word made flesh.'

He was the singular, true voice of God, in human form, during the thirty-three years of His earthly stay.

His appearance was an amazing experience for the Jewish people as they had not heard the voice of God for well over four hundred years, not since the prophet Malachi.

However, what was the situation once Jesus had ascended and he was no longer 'the Word in the flesh'?

How did the early Church hear His voice after that?

It seems very clear that the Holy Spirit, by which the first Christians were empowered on the day of Pentecost, was a major factor in determining how believers were to hear the voice of Christ, as the Head of His Church.

Pentecost was significant as it was a fulfilment of what Jesus had predicted about the future source of their spiritual learning, guidance, and authority.

In three specific ways He had declared the role of the Holy Spirit:

He said:

> "But the Comforter, which is the Holy Ghost, whom the Father will send in my name, he shall teach you all things, and bring all things to your remembrance, whatsoever I have said unto you." (John 14:26).

He went on to say:

> "But when the Comforter is come, whom I will send unto you from the Father, even the Spirit of truth, which proceedeth from the Father, he shall testify of me." (John 15:26).

And once more, Jesus affirms:

> "But when the Spirit of truth comes, He will guide you into all truth. For He will not speak on His own authority. But He will speak whatever He hears, and He will tell you things that are to come." (John 16:13)

Jesus declared clearly that it was the Holy Spirit who would teach them, remind them, testify about Him, guide them into all truth, and relay details of important future events.

What is also significant is that Peter, on the Day of Pentecost, points to Joel's prophecy and confirms some of the ways, in which the Holy Spirit would speak to believers going forward:

> "In the last days it shall be,' says God, 'that I will pour out My Spirit on all flesh; your sons and your daughters shall prophesy, your young men shall see visions, and your old men shall dream dreams. Even on My menservants and maidservants, I will pour out My Spirit in those days and they shall prophesy." (Acts 2:17-18)

So, do we see evidence of how the Holy Spirit became the pivotal way by which the purpose and will of God were conveyed to and through the Church?

Let us look at some examples of where and how we see that happening.

> Acts 8:29: "The Spirit said to Philip, "Go to this chariot and stay with it."

> Acts 10:19-20: "While Peter thought about the vision, the Spirit said to him, "Three men are looking for you. So, rise and go down, and go with them, doubting nothing. For I have sent them."

> Acts 11:12: "And immediately three men sent from Caesarea to me came to the house where I was. The Spirit told me to go with them, without hesitation."

> Acts 11:28: "One of them, named Agabus, stood up and prophesied by the Spirit that there would be a great famine throughout all the world, which came to pass in the days of Claudius Caesar."

> Acts 16:7: "When they came near Mysia, they tried to go into Bithynia, but the Spirit did not allow them."

Acts 16:9: "During the night a vision appeared to Paul: A man of Macedonia stood and pleaded with him, saying, "Come over to Macedonia and help us."

Acts 18:6: "When Paul had laid his hands on them, the Holy Spirit came on them, and they spoke in other tongues and prophesied."

Acts 21:10 "......and (we) entered the house of Philip the evangelist, who was one of the seven, and stayed with him. He had four virgin daughters who prophesied."

So, we see that there is a lot of evidence of how the Holy Spirit connected directly with the early Church and with individual believers, speaking to them and providing insight, information, guidance, and empowerment.

There are also numerous other incidents, where even angels appeared, to the apostles and other believers, also providing them with direction and support.

So, what of the Church today?

We certainly need to heed the example of the early Church and pay particular attention to just how prevalent the role of the Holy Spirit was.

Joel's prophecy is as relevant now, as it was on the Day of Pentecost:

"'In the last days it shall be,' says God, 'that I will pour out My Spirit on all flesh; your sons and your daughters shall prophesy, your young men shall see visions, and your old men shall dream dreams."

"Even on My menservants and maidservants I will pour out My Spirit in those days, and they shall prophesy. And I will show wonders in heaven above and signs on the earth below: blood, and fire, and vapor of smoke."

"The sun shall be turned into darkness, and the moon into blood, before that great and glorious

day of the Lord comes. And whoever calls on the
name of the Lord shall be saved" (Acts 2:17-21)

Joel's prophecy still holds good as we are still living in the last
days, when I last looked!

## CHAPTER THIRTY

# Hearing the Spirit's Voice

**A**ll true believers can hear the voice of the Holy Spirit. Jesus said, definitively:

> "My sheep hear My voice, and I know them, and they follow Me." (John 10:27)

The problem we have, frequently, is that there is interference from every other voice coming to us from a myriad of different sources.

In these circumstances, the voice of the Holy Spirit becomes easily "drowned out" by a cacophony of these other distracting voices. Our spiritual focus, and subsequent actions and behaviour, then become unduly affected by those influences that are not emanating directly from the Holy Spirit.

Sounds familiar?

Isaiah's words are very appropriate:

> "Incline your ear, and come to Me. Listen, so that your soul may live" (Isaiah 55:3)

We need to be available and to stay attuned to the Holy Spirit and be open to His voice and direction. The consequences of not staying attuned to the Holy Spirit and failing to 'abide' in faith are potentially dangerous for us.

Look at what Jesus says:

> "Those along the path are those who hear. Then comes the devil, who takes away the word from their hearts, lest they should believe and be saved." (Luke 8:12).

Remember that the Greek word for 'saved' here is 'sozo' and means much more than just being born again. It is also about our ongoing protection and preservation as believers – physically and spiritually.

Our determination, to hear His voice and stand upon His promises, in every situation, is of paramount importance.

A familiar example of how these external distractions damage us is when Peter walked on the water to get to Jesus.

He had already received a positive response from Jesus to his question as he saw Him walking on the water towards him:

> "Lord if it be you, bid me come unto thee on the water" (Matthew 14:28)

Jesus encouraged him to leave the safety of the boat and walk towards Him.

Peter had the Word of Jesus.

However, he did not make it all the way, because he was distracted by other external factors.

The effect of those distractions is what caused him to start to sink:

> "And when Peter got out of the boat, he walked on the water to go to Jesus. But when he saw the strong wind, he was afraid, and beginning to sink, he cried out, "Lord, save me!" (Matthew 14:29-30)

Both Jesus and the early Church were attuned to the voice and influence of the Holy Spirit.

The early Church, especially, was surrounded constantly by distractions which could have easily diverted them away from God's will and purpose.

Among the most obvious was violent religious persecution from the Jewish community and dangerous, political pressure from the occupying Romans – life-threatening, in both cases.

In these circumstances, they were completely dependent on the voice of direction and guidance that only came from the Holy Spirit to protect them, guide them, direct them, and above all, energise their ministry.

John reassures the Church of Jesus today, as he reassured

believers, across the early Church:

> "But the anointing which you have received from Him remains in you, and you do not need anyone to teach you. For as the same anointing teaches you concerning all things, and is truth, and is no lie, and just as it has taught you, remain in Him." (1 John 2:27)

## CHAPTER THIRTY-ONE

# Be Led by the Spirit

We saw in the previous chapter, that even though Peter had the word of Jesus which encouraged him to step out of the boat, he still lost focus on that word and began to sink.

A key part of our walk with Christ is not only hearing the voice of the Holy Spirit but also acting on that word with confidence and with faith and maintaining that confidence in the face of challenges and distractions.

This step of faith is an act of will and boldness, which allows the Holy Spirit to enact the promise of God in our lives.

As James says:

> "As the body without the spirit is dead, so faith without works is dead." (James 2:26)

Paul adds to James' insight:

> "For as many as are led by the Spirit of God, these are the sons of God." (Romans 8:14)

An experience that I had not too long ago helped me understand much more clearly what Paul was highlighting here. It is a simple, but helpful, example of why we need to constantly ensure we remain attuned to the voice and the leading of the Holy Spirit.

A while ago I drove to my daughter's new home in Weymouth, UK. I needed the help of some additional guidance to find my way.

My car, at that time, was a little on the elderly side and its GPS relied on data that had been installed a few years back and therefore did not account for any new road systems constructed in more recent years.

Even though the GPS helped me most of the way, there came a point when my ancient GPS told me suddenly that I was actually in the middle of some fields, even though there was a new, modern bypass system in front of me.

What was I to do? I was clearly lost and had no idea which direction to take, after a lot of trial and error, and no small amount of frustration, I did eventually arrive!

As we grow in the things of God, there will be many times when we find ourselves in that very unfamiliar and challenging territory.

Our inbuilt "natural" instincts and experience can frequently turn out to be little help and "leaning on our own understanding" will likely lead to frustration and unnecessary anxiety.

These situations can appear problematic but are frequently God-given opportunities to seek out the guidance of the Holy Spirit and discover the direction we need to be taking.

The Holy Spirit's "software" never needs updating, and His GPS is always accurate and up to date.

We are called by God, to be led continuously by the Holy Spirit as a part of our daily walk with Jesus.

This walk in the Spirit marks us out from the world and provides us with access to the complete navigational resources of God.

Let us heed the words of Solomon:

> "In all your ways acknowledge Him and He shall direct your paths" (Proverbs 3:6)

## CHAPTER THIRTY-TWO

# The Authority of the Name of Jesus

A s believers, we elevate and praise the name of the Lord! We also know that there is power, authority, and protection, in the name of Jesus.

Jeremiah declares:

> "There is no one like You, O Lord. You are great, and Your name is great in might." (Jeremiah 10:6)

The book of Proverbs tells us:

> "The name of the Lord is a strong tower; the righteous man runs into it and is safe." (Proverbs 18:10)

Paul makes the name of Jesus all-encompassing when writing to the church in Colossae:

> "And whatever you do in word or deed, do all in the name of the Lord Jesus, giving thanks to God the Father through Him." (Colossians 3:17)

So, what is the significance of doing anything in the name of something or someone?

Well, it depends on what or who that name represents, and it also depends on the power and authority that is vested in that name.

If someone knocks on your door and just tells you their name, it going to means very little in terms of actual authority, however, if they then tell you they are calling, 'in the name of King Charles the Third', their presence and authority takes on a new meaning and authority.

That nondescript person standing in your doorway now represents the monarchy of Great Britain with all its inherent power, influence, and authority.

A name, then, represents either a person or an entity and all the authority vested in them.

When we understand the power and authority that is invested in Jesus Himself, we can then grasp the level of authority that His Name represents.

What is the level of Jesus' overall authority and power?

Here is what Jesus said of Himself:

> "All authority in heaven and on earth has been given to me." (Matthew 28:18)

That level of authority covers just about everything and everybody.

So, what does the Father say about His Son's declaration?

> "For it pleased the Father that in Him (Jesus) all fullness should dwell, and to reconcile all things to Himself by Him, having made peace through the blood of His cross, by Him, I say—whether they are things in earth or things in heaven." (Colossians 1:19-20)

Jesus said it and the Father endorsed it, which makes His authority and power, an eternal fact.

The name of Jesus, then, carries universal power and total authority, both in Heaven and on Earth.

So, what's the consequence of Christ's authority on His Church?

Well, His Church is like an embassy, Christ's embassy on earth. He is the Head of State but is no longer physically on this earth.

Paul tells us where he is located:

> "If you then were raised with Christ, desire those things which are above, where Christ sits at the right hand of God." (Colossians 3:1)

The Church then, like an embassy, represents Christ and His Kingdom here on this earth and we, the Body of Christ, are His ambassadors.

Paul says:

> "We are ambassadors for Christ, as though God were pleading through us" (2 Corinthians 5:20)

On one occasion, Paul described himself as an 'ambassador in chains.' (Ephesians 6:20)

Like embassy officials, Christian believers, although located here on this earth, do not belong here as they are citizens of another country.

Jesus says that of us:

> "They are not of the world, even as I am not of the world "(John 17:16)

Paul adds:

> "Now, therefore, you are no longer strangers and foreigners, but are fellow citizens with the saints and members of the household of God" (Ephesians 2:19)

We are located in this world, but we are not its citizens. So, we can now see why Paul said:

> "And whatever you do in word or deed, do all in the name of the Lord Jesus, giving thanks to God the Father through Him." ((Colossians 3:17)

We use His Name because everything we carry out in this life is as Christ's authorised representatives, we are his embassy officials, and we carry out our spiritual responsibilities in His Name.

However, is His Name just an important figurehead, or does the name of Jesus carry real authority?

The Scriptures point to the name of Jesus as carrying true authority and being far more than just a notional identity.

Jesus himself declared to His disciples:

> "If you ask anything in My name, I will do it". (John 14:14)

He foretold that Christians would enjoy divine protection and spiritual authority in His Name:

"These signs will accompany those who believe: In My name, they will cast out demons; they will speak with new tongues; they will take up serpents; if they drink any deadly thing, it will not hurt them; they will lay hands on the sick, and they will recover." (Mark 16:17-18)

We can also see the extent to which the early Church implemented and used the name of Jesus in their ministry of the Gospel. Salvation is secured in His Name:

"There is no salvation in any other, for there is no other name under heaven given among men by which we must be saved." (Acts 4:12)

Repentance and Water Baptism were carried out in His Name:

"Repent and be baptized, every one of you, in the name of Jesus Christ for the forgiveness of sins" (Acts 2:38)

Healing was carried out in His Name:

"And His name, by faith in His name, has made this man strong, whom you see and know. And faith which comes through Him has given him perfect health in your presence." (Acts 3:16).

We can see clearly from these examples how the Name of Jesus carries, with it, total authority over all things, in Heaven and Earth.

We, then as Spirit-filled believers, represent Christ and have, by faith, access to all that His Name represents.

We should continuously embrace all that the name of Jesus represents and stand upon its total God-given authority.

"Therefore, God highly exalted Him and gave Him the name, which is above every name, that at the name of Jesus every knee should bow, of those in heaven and on earth and under the earth, and every tongue should confess that Jesus Christ is Lord, to the glory of God the Father" (Philippians 2:9-11)

## CHAPTER THIRTY-THREE

# The Power of Praise!

Praising God is most frequently encouraged and proclaimed, in the book of Psalms.

The Psalmist writes about praising God over one hundred and fifty times, which gives you a reasonably clear indication of how important he believed it was. It's also significant that the psalmist talks frequently, in terms of "I will......" when it comes to praising God.

> "I will thank the Lord according to His righteousness and will sing praise to the name of the Lord Most High" (Psalm 7:17)

> "I will declare Your name to my community; in the midst of the congregation, I will praise You" (Psalm 22:22).

He sees the praising of God as a willing choice.

He makes the positive decision to consistently open his heart and mind, in gratitude and praise to God, for His goodness and His love:

> "I will bless the Lord at all times; His praise will continually be in my mouth. My soul will make its boast in the Lord; the humble will hear of it and be glad." (Psalm 34:1-2)

Not only does the Psalmist see praising God as a priority for himself, but also a priority for the people of God.

He declares, in effect, that the community of God's people should see praising Him, as a highly appropriate thing to do, and ensure that it's carried out in a very audible manner:

> "Rejoice in the Lord, O you righteous, for praise is fitting for the upright" (Psalm 33:1)

> "Oh, bless our God, you people, and make the voice of His praise to be heard" (Psalm 66:8)

The Psalmist, is also a great believer, that an array of musical instruments should accompany His people's offering of praise and thanksgiving to God:

> "Praise the Lord with the harp; Make melody to Him with an instrument of ten strings" (Psalm 33:2)

He also sees the need for praising God to be a noisy, joyful musical outpouring:

> "Make a joyful noise unto the Lord, all the earth: make a loud noise, and rejoice, and sing praise. Sing unto the Lord with the harp, with the harp, and the voice of a psalm. With trumpets and sound of cornet make a joyful noise before the Lord, the King" (Psalm 98:46)

> "Let them praise His name with dancing; let them sing praises unto Him with the tambourine and harp" (Psalm 149:3)

What about Dancing?
Well, we read in 2 Samuel 6:14 that:

> "David danced before the Lord with all of his might...."

This whole desire and energy to praise God is seen as a joyful and willing offering to Him, in loud praise, with music, with instruments, and even with dance.

He describes it as a special kind of spiritual sacrifice, that we willingly and joyfully offer to Him, whatever the circumstances:

> "I will offer to You the sacrifice of thanksgiving and will call upon the name of the Lord". (Psalm 116:17)

He states that praising God is a priority, even at a time of great need and stress:

> "Why art thou cast down, O my soul? and why art thou disquieted within me? Hope thou in God: for I shall yet praise him, who is the health of my countenance, and my God" (Psalm 42:11).

And what is God's response to us praising Him at all times?

> "But You are holy, O You who inhabits the praises of Israel" (Psalm 22:3)

The psalmist declares that God dwells and abides in our praises of Him.

The Hebrew here for 'inhabits' is 'yâshab' which can mean 'to sit down', what a wonderful way to describe His Presence with us. God sits down, and relaxes, in the middle of this noisy, musical expression of love and gratefulness from His people.

It is no wonder that the Lord will also reveal more of Himself and the power of His salvation to those whose mouths are honest and whose hearts are filled with praise to God:

> "Whoso offers praise glorifies me: and to him that orders his conversation aright will I shew the salvation of God." (Psalm 50:23).

So how does all this wonderful encouragement to praise God translate itself into the early Church and into our lives today? Were they more sedate in their gatherings? Should we be a little more conservative?

Praising God and Christ is highly visible in the New Testament church and without any noticeable difference to how the Psalmist described and encouraged it.

Praising Him becomes even more prevalent, even more enthusiastic, and equally as musical.

Like the psalmist, Paul advocates a continuous sacrifice of praise to God:

> "Through Him, then, let us continually offer to God the sacrifice of praise, which is the fruit of our

lips, giving thanks to His name." (Hebrews 13:15)

The musical accompaniment continues as well:

> "Speak to one another in psalms, hymns, and spiritual songs, singing and making melody in your heart to the Lord." (Ephesians 5:19)

And what about praising God in difficult and challenging circumstances?

Let us take a look at Paul and Barnabas, bruised and beaten and imprisoned in Philippi:

> "At midnight Paul and Silas were praying and singing hymns to God, and the prisoners were listening to them. Suddenly there was a great earthquake, so that the foundations of the prison were shaken. And immediately all the doors were opened, and everyone's shackles were loosened" (Acts 16:25-26)

God 'sat down' with them in prison and an earthquake ensued!

Let us follow these examples and incorporate more praise, more thanks, and more rejoicing into our lives- individually and in our gatherings.

> "Let the word of Christ dwell in you richly in all wisdom, teaching and admonishing one another in psalms and hymns and spiritual songs, singing with grace in your hearts to the Lord." (Colossians 3:16)

## CHAPTER THIRTY-FOUR

# The Authority of the Believer

At the time of creation, God made a very important statement about the function and role of mankind immediately before Adam and Eve were themselves created.

God defined their role and relationship, as it pertained to creation as a whole.

He said:

> "Let us make man in our image, after our likeness, and let them have dominion over the fish of the sea, and over the birds of the air, and the livestock, and all the earth, and over every creeping thing that creeps on the earth." (Genesis 1:26)

The Hebrew word for 'dominion' is 'radah,' meaning to reign over, to subjugate, or to govern.

We would probably see this as meaning, something similar to a monarch reigning over a kingdom with control and authority.

So, from the very commencement of time, we see God's intention, in respect of all that He had created.

Humanity was created and placed in the centre of everything that God had created, with overall authority and control.

When Adam and Eve sinned and were expelled from Eden, that position and authority were completely eradicated.

God's punishment was spelled out:

> "Cursed is the ground on account of you; in hard labour you will eat of it all the days of your life. Thorns and thistles, it will bring forth for you, and

you will eat the plants of the field. By the sweat of
your face, you will eat bread" (Genesis 3:17-19)

Following the Fall, the original authority that humanity had
over creation was rarely seen, other than in some unique situations,
designated by God himself.

Moses parting the Red Sea, Joshua halting the sun and Elijah
calling down fire are probably better-known examples of chosen
men of God, who demonstrated authority over creation.

It was not until Jesus arrived in human form, that we see that
original authority and dominion over creation demonstrated again.

Jesus turned water into wine, walked on the waters of the Sea
of Galilee, calmed a raging storm, and directed experienced, but
frustrated fishermen, where to cast their nets. He even cursed a fig
tree and it perished.

Jesus also demonstrated dominion over demonic forces, sick-
ness, and disease:

> "In the evening, when the sun had set, they brought
> to Him all who were sick and those who were pos-
> sessed with demons. The whole city was gathered at
> the door, and He healed many who were sick with
> various diseases and cast out many demons." (Mark
> 1:32-34)

We also see Him, delegating this authority, to His disciples:

> "And he called the twelve together and gave them
> power and authority over all demons and to cure
> diseases." (Luke 9:1)

> "Behold, I have given you authority to tread on ser-
> pents and scorpions, and over all the power of the
> enemy, and nothing shall hurt you." (Luke 10:19).

This delegation of authority was a very strong indicator of what
was to come for His Church, and He stated as much:

> "Truly, truly I say to you, he who believes in Me
> will do the works that I do also. And he will do
> greater works than these because I am going to My
> Father" (John 14:12)

What was the significance of His ascending to His Father?

> "Nevertheless, I tell you the truth: It is expedient for you that I go away. For if I do not go away, the Comforter will not come to you" (John 16:7)

On the day of Pentecost, the promised Comforter arrived, and the apostles were then empowered, just as Jesus was during His earthly ministry.

They carried the same authority and power that He had possessed, during His earthly ministry.

So, how was that authority demonstrated in the early Church?

> "Believers were increasingly added to the Lord, crowds of both men and women, so believers were increasingly added to the Lord, crowds of both men and women so that they even brought the sick out into the streets and placed them on beds and mats, that at least the shadow of Peter passing by might touch some of them."

> "Crowds also came out of the cities surrounding Jerusalem, bringing the sick and those who were afflicted by evil spirits, and they were all healed. that they even brought the sick out into the streets and placed them on beds and mats, that at least the shadow of Peter passing by might touch some of them." (Acts 5:14-15)

We also know that Paul demonstrated supernatural power and authority:

> "Therefore they (Paul and Barnabas) stayed there a long time, speaking boldly in the Lord, who was bearing witness to the word of His grace, granting signs and wonders to be done by their hands." (Acts 14:3)

Following his shipwreck, Paul was bitten by a viper:

> "But he shook off the creature into the fire and suffered no harm" (Acts 28:5)

We can see clearly that the authority and power ordained by God in His original creation plan were lost by Adam's sin.

However, we also see it restored by Jesus, and transferred by the Holy Spirit to His Church, His Body.

We, as Spirit-filled believers, can now embrace by faith, the totality of His authority and His provision, as His New Creation.

Let us possess what God has provided for us, to take our place as members of His Church, empowered by the Holy Spirit, with spiritual authority.

> "For though we walk in the flesh, we are not waging war according to the flesh. For the weapons of our warfare are not of the flesh but have divine power to destroy strongholds, casting down imaginations and every high thing that exalts itself against the knowledge of God, bringing every thought into captivity to the obedience of Christ". (2 Corinthians 10:3-5)

## CHAPTER THIRTY-FIVE

# The Fruit of the Spirit

"But the fruit of the Spirit is love, joy, peace, patience, gentleness, goodness, faith, meekness, and self-control; against such there is no law." (Galatians 5:22-23)

A minister friend of mine shared this little piece of spiritual insight with me a while ago, and I found it very helpful.

He said that the fruit of the Spirit reflected the life of Christ, and the gifts of the Spirit reflected the ministry of Christ.

This wonderful piece of insight shows just how the Holy Spirit energises and empowers the Body of Christ so that we, His Body, can demonstrate to the world, the fullness and completeness of Christ.

Each one of us contributes to sharing that fullness of Christ within the Body of Christ and beyond, by living and ministering as the Holy Spirit leads us, directs us, and empowers us.

However, there is one important thing we need to fully understand, at this point, and that is the phrase, 'of the Spirit'.

This phrase highlights, that it is the life and nature of Christ within us that becomes visible as 'fruit' and can then be experienced by those around us.

Paul puts it this way:

> "But we have this treasure in earthen vessels, the excellency of the power being from God and not from ourselves" (2 Corinthians 4:7)

These fruits of the Spirit are not essentially human qualities or human characteristics, they are the divine qualities and divine characteristics of Christ Himself, revealed in and through us.

Paul describes these manifestations of Christ, as being like a spiritual fragrance:

"For we are to God a sweet fragrance of Christ among those who are saved and among those who perish" (2 Corinthians 2:14)

What makes all this possible is that Christ not only lives within us but that we are also connected and united with Him.

As Paul writes:

"But he who is joined to the Lord becomes one spirit with Him" (1 Corinthians 6:17)

So, the fruits of the Spirit, are a manifestation of the life of Christ within us, permeating out through our earthly being and impacting those around us, with the very presence and nature of Christ Himself.

What are these fruits of the Spirit?

Let us look at each one in turn, starting with 'Love'.

'Love' is agape love, which is the unconditional love of God and is His very core nature.

This is the quality of love that enables us to "love our enemies, to bless those who curse us, do good to those who hate us, and pray for those who spitefully use us and persecute us."

This is the love that Jesus demonstrated on the Cross when He said:

"Father, forgive them for they know not what they do" (Luke 23:34)

Similarly, it is that same love expressed by Stephen, as he was stoned to death:

"Lord, lay not this sin to their charge" (Acts 7:60)

It's that unconditional love of God Himself, which never seeks a reward or any recompense.

Do we have access to that kind of love?

Yes, we do!

Paul describes this love as being, "shed abroad in our hearts by the Holy Ghost" (Romans 5:5)

The next fruit of the Spirit is 'Joy', which Nehemiah describes as "our strength" (Nehemiah 8:10)

This is the same joy of the Lord, which sustained and delivered Paul and Silas, when they found themselves imprisoned, in appalling circumstances, in Philippi.

Like them, this joy of the Spirit enables us to give thanks and praise to God, in every situation and circumstance, however challenging.

The psalmist reassures us:

> "You will make known to me the path of life; in Your presence is fullness of joy; at Your right hand there are pleasures for evermore" (Psalms 16:11)

The psalmist again declares:

> "I will also clothe her priests with salvation: and her saints shall shout aloud for joy" (Psalm 132:16)

The next gift of the Spirit is 'Peace'.
Paul encourages the Philippians,

> 'And the peace of God, which surpasses all understanding, and will protect your hearts and minds through Christ Jesus." (Philippians 4:7)

> This encouragement from Paul expresses so clearly the supernatural qualities of this 'heavenly' peace which defies logic and provides total security from threats of every kind.

This is the peace of God, which thrives in times of confusion and chaos when human anxieties and fears arise and try to dominate us.

This is the peace of God, which is within us and can speak into every chaotic situation and say, as Jesus said to the storm, 'Peace, be still.'

Isaiah puts it this way:

> "You will keep him in perfect peace, whose mind is stayed on You because he trusts in You." (Isaiah 26:3)

The psalmist echoes Isaiah's words:

"I will both lay me down in peace and sleep: for thou
Lord only makest me dwell in safety". (Psalm 4:8)

Next comes, 'Patience'.

This is the patience that 'waits patiently for the Lord', especially in times of negative circumstances, challenging situations, and great difficulties, when a response from God is not immediately forthcoming.

As the psalmist said:

"I waited patiently for the Lord, and he inclined
unto me and heard my cry" (Psalm 40:1)

This is the patience that tells us not to 'lean on our own understanding', but to rest confidently in Him, relying totally on His faithfulness and provision.

James also emphasises the underlying necessity for us as believers to display patience:

"But let patience have her perfect work, that you
might be perfect and entire, wanting nothing"
(James 1:4)

Paul reassures the Colossians that, as believers, we are:

"Strengthened with all might, according to his
mighty power unto all patience...." (Colossians
1:11)

'Gentleness' is that fruit of the Spirit, which enables us to 'live peaceably with all men.' (Romans 12:18)

David made a wonderful statement about the nature and result of demonstrating gentleness:

"Thou hast given me the shield of thy salvation:
and thy gentleness has made me great" (2 Samuel
22:36)

In the face of persecution, conflict, and chaos, the
gentleness of the Spirit enables us to be 'quick to
hear, slow to speak and slow to anger.' (James 1:19)

As Jesus, the great role model of gentleness, said:

> "Take My yoke upon you, and learn from Me. For I am meek and lowly in heart, and you will find rest for your souls. (Matthew 11:29)

Paul underlines these words of Jesus:

> "With all humility, meekness, and patience, bearing with one another in love." (Ephesians 4:2)

The fruit of 'Goodness' of the Spirit, enables us to give and to share unconditionally.

When confronted by greed, selfishness, and inconsideration, the goodness of God causes us to give and give again, without ever looking for any reward or compensation.

Goodness and unconditional sharing were a clear feature of the early Church:

> "There was no one among them who lacked, for all those who were owners of land or houses sold them, and brought the income from what was sold, and placed it at the apostles' feet. And it was distributed to each according to his need." (Acts 4:34-35)

Paul exhorted the church in Galatia:

> "Therefore, as we have opportunity, let us do good to all people, especially to those who are of the household of faith." (Galatians 6:10)

He goes on to commend the church in Rome:

> "Now I am persuaded concerning you, my brothers, that you also are full of goodness, filled with all knowledge, and also able to instruct one another. (Romans 15:14)

Paul again emphasises the power of goodness as a fruit of the Spirit:

> "Do not be overcome by evil but overcome evil with good." (Romans 12:21)

Faith is the next fruit of the Spirit.

The word 'faith' here is probably better defined as 'faithfulness'.

Faithfulness in Christian believers would flow from an absolute trust in the faithfulness of God Himself, the inherent truth of His Word, and the reliability of His promises.

Paul describes God's faithfulness like this:

> "For all the promises of God are yea, and in Him
> Amen, unto the glory of God by us" (2 Corinthians
> 2:10)

As believers, we say "Yes!" to God and "Amen!" to His promises because we know He is faithful!

Paul again stresses his confidence in the faithfulness of God as a result of his relationship with Christ:

> "For these things I suffer, but I am not ashamed, for
> I know whom I have believed, and am persuaded
> that He is able to keep that which I have commit-
> ted to Him until that Day". (2 Corinthians 1;12)

Faithfulness as a fruit of the Spirit is demonstrated in a Christian believer by a strong and consistent trust in the absolute reliability of God and His word.

As a result, their lives will reflect spiritual stability, inner strength, and personal integrity stemming from their close walk and relationship with Jesus.

As Proverbs says so concisely:

> "Let not steadfast love and faithfulness forsake
> you; bind them around your neck; write them on
> the tablet of your heart. So, you will find favour
> and good success in the sight of God and man."
> (Proverbs 3:3-4)

Meekness is the fruit of the Spirit, which always seeks to avoid harshness or abrasiveness in words, behaviour, and, above all, in our relationships.

Meekness of the Spirit is slow to temper, not given to anger, and seeks a mutual resolution in any disagreement, without compromising God's truth in the process.

As Peter admonishes us:

> "But let it be the hidden nature of the heart, that which is not corruptible, even the ornament of a gentle and quiet spirit, which is very precious in the sight of God" (1 Peter 3:4)

The psalmist adds in reassurance:

> "The Lord lifts up the meek; He casts the wicked down to the ground" (Psalm 147:6)

Finally, Self-control is the fruit of the Spirit that Solomon says, makes us, spiritually strong.

Proverbs says:

> "He who is slow to anger is better than the mighty, and he who rules his spirit than he who takes a city." (Proverbs 16:32)

Self-control enables us to remain in God's rest and not give way to arrogance, anger, or bitterness which can defile us spiritually.

Peter admonishes us all:

> "The end of all things is at hand, therefore be self-controlled and sober-minded for the sake of your prayers." (1 Peter 4:7)

Proverbs again, this time, warning us:

> "He who has no rule over his own spirit is like a city that is broken down and without walls" (Proverbs 25:28).

Let us remind ourselves again, that these fruits of the Spirit are not human qualities or human characteristics but that they are the divine qualities and characteristics of Christ Himself, revealed through us by the Holy Spirit.

Let us heed the words of Jesus and allow the Holy Spirit to flow through us, enabling us to bear fruit that reflects Christ Himself and bring glory to God.

> "Remain in Me, as I also remain in you. As the

branch cannot bear fruit by itself unless it remains in the vine, neither can you, unless you remain in Me. I am the Vine, and you are the branches. He who remains in Me, and I in him, bears much fruit. For without Me, you can do nothing" (John 15:4-5)

# CHAPTER THIRTY-SIX

# Trial by Fire

T here are occasions in our walk with Christ when we are going to be seriously challenged, these challenges, frequently come in the form of life situations, which can sometimes, threaten to overwhelm us completely.

It is then, we have to energise our fellowship with Christ, by spending quality time in prayer and accessing by faith, His amazing provision.

Paul admonishes us to:

> "Be anxious for nothing, but in everything, by prayer and supplication with gratitude, make your requests known to God. And the peace of God, which surpasses all understanding, will protect your hearts and minds through Christ Jesus." (Philippians 4:67)

However, there are those situations that can and will arise, that challenge our very commitment to Christ. These situations can demand us to make decisions, about our Christian faith, which is momentous and potentially, life changing.

As the current world becomes darker and the negative pressures on our Christian faith surface almost daily, we are going to be increasingly challenged to stand firm in our commitment and obedience to Christ.

Going forward, the Church will have to be more prepared than ever, to demonstrate its total trust in Christ, in the face of an increasingly godless and threatening world.

Tribulation and persecution are certainly well underway, in some parts of the world. In those situations, God's people have to make very tough choices about their faith in Christ. The consequences of those choices can be life-threatening, and sometimes even terminal.

There is a great need today, to embrace the words that Jesus used to reassure His disciples because he knew, they would face intense persecution, as they took the Gospel out into the world.

He said this to them:

> "I have said these things to you, that in me you may have peace. In the world you will have tribulation. But take heart; I have overcome the world." (John 16:33)

Two examples in the Scriptures are very familiar to most Christians, but whose message is now so compelling and so relevant.

Throughout the Scriptures, there are those whose commitment to God stands out as an example to us all, both in terms of their obedience and their total trust in His protection and His support.

Daniel was such a man - he was a prophet of God and a man of continuous prayer.

Because of his commitment to God, he had prospered and been honoured by his king, Darius, above all the other high officials because an 'excellent spirit' was in him. The king had also planned to promote him again and to expand his responsibilities to cover the whole of Persia.

However, Daniel was about to be challenged, and that challenge would be potentially life-threatening in its implications.

Darius' other high officials, filled with jealousy and malice, created a situation where Daniel was, by law, forbidden to pray openly to God. The punishment, for breaking that law, was death.

Daniel, however, stood firm and in the face of certain death, refused to comply with this corrupt law, essentially designed to destroy him. He was resolute and would not compromise his faith.

He refused to yield to fear and was prepared to die, rather than disobey God.

King Darius could do nothing to save Daniel as once a Persian law had been signed it could not be repealed.

"Then the king commanded, and they brought Daniel and cast him into the den of lions" (Daniel 6:16)

When the king visited the lions' den the next morning, he was prepared for the worst.

However, we know that God rewarded Daniel's obedience, his faith, and his commitment.

> "Then Daniel said to the king, "O king, live forever! My God has sent His angel and has shut the lions' mouths so that they have not hurt me because innocence was found in me before Him; and also, before you, O king, I have done no harm." (Daniel 6:21-22)

In our second example, the Babylonian emperor, Nebuchadnezzar, a tyrant, who had destroyed Jerusalem, and taken the Israelites captive, had built a golden statue in the plain of Dura.

He had further commanded all his government officials to bow down and worship it and any of them, who failed to comply with his outrageous edict, would be killed by being thrown into a blazing furnace.

Certain of Nebuchadnezzar's officials, informed the king that the three Jewish officials, Shadrach, Meshach, and Abednego, whom the king had already appointed to high office in Babylon, were refusing to worship the golden statue.

The three Jewish officials were hastily brought before Nebuchadnezzar, where they defiantly told the king that they had no intention of worshipping his image, they informed the king that they would serve and worship the one true God of Israel, and to that end, would take their punishment in the fiery furnace.

Like Daniel, they too, would not compromise their faith, they too refused to yield to fear, and they too were prepared to die rather than disobey God.

Nebuchadnezzar became angry and commanded that they be thrown into the fiery furnace and instructed for the furnace to be heated seven times hotter than normal.

However, when the king looked what he saw were four people, not three, walking unharmed in the flames and, it's said that the fourth figure was "like a son of God."

Seeing this phenomenon, Nebuchadnezzar, immediately had the three men brought out of the furnace. He then discovered that the fire had not had any effect on their bodies at all, the hair of their heads was not singed, their cloaks were not harmed, and there was no smell of fire on them.

Like Daniel, God had delivered them in the most challenging of situations, because of their obedience to Him and their immovable faith in His protection.

The message to all of us as believers is clear.

Whatever the future holds for Christian believers, one thing is for sure and that is, that it will be as challenging and as confrontational as it was for Daniel and his three Jewish compatriots.

So, let us embrace Peter's reassurance:

"Beloved, do not be surprised at the fiery trial when it comes upon you to test you, as though something strange were happening to you. But rejoice as far as you share Christ's sufferings, that you may also rejoice and be glad when his glory is revealed. If you are insulted for the name of Christ, you are blessed, because the Spirit of glory and of God rests upon you. "(1 Peter 4:12-14)

CHAPTER THIRTY-SEVEN

# Testing and Sifting

"And the Lord said, Simon, Simon, behold, Satan hath desired to have you, that he may sift you as wheat: But I have prayed for thee, that thy faith fail not: and when thou art converted, strengthen thy brethren." (Luke 22:31-32)

These verses are quite incredible when you consider what Jesus was saying to Peter. Jesus described to Peter, Satan's desire to test him, personally.

Satan believed that he could break Peter's faith and his commitment to Christ and had requested that he be allowed to put him to the test. Satan saw an opportunity to stymie God's plan and purpose because Peter had already been chosen by Jesus to lead the Church after He had returned to heaven.

However, Jesus was confident that Peter was strong and resilient enough to withstand Satan's head-on attack. Jesus reassured Peter that He had prayed for him, "that his faith fails not".

"Sifting as wheat" here reflects what is known as "winnowing", a farming process designed to separate and remove unneeded chaff from the more valuable grain.

Here, the sifting process is applied to the testing of Peter's faith and commitment to Christ.

The testing or sifting process was intended to separate away, like chaff, those parts of Peter's life and character that were weaknesses and obstacles to God's will, at the same time, as weaknesses were being diminished, other personal attributes were being strengthened.

Those being strengthened were those things that were of prime importance to the purpose of God going forward - his faith and his total commitment to Jesus.

It is interesting here to note, that so often Satan is seen as a spiritual predator, and needing to be constantly rebuked or cast out, however, here Satan is positioned as a tool, in the hand of God.

On this occasion, Satan was being used by God as a tool to enable Peter's maturity and preparation for his future role, in leading the Church.

There is no evidence, that Jesus was ever prepared to spare Peter from this challenging experience. We know that Jesus Himself had been tested in the wilderness, and He knew that Peter too, had to be tested.

What did Jesus know about Peter's faith, which would have given him the confidence that Peter was up to the challenge?

What we do know is that Peter had already made two very important and insightful statements to Jesus.

These two statements reflected the depth of insight, and faith, that Peter possessed about Jesus - who he was, and the life-giving nature of his teaching.

When Jesus had asked his disciples, who men said they thought He was, it was Peter who said, "Thou art the Christ, the Son of the Living God." (Matthew 16:16)

Later, when several of Jesus' disciples decided not to follow Him, it was Peter who declared that he would stay, declaring to Jesus:

"To whom shall we go? You have the words of eternal life." (John 6:68)

None of the other disciples, had such clear and strong insight about Jesus, as Peter did, and Jesus was aware of it. Jesus also knew that this degree of insight and personal faith, needed to be contained in a strong and resilient vessel.

He knew from his own experience, that this chosen vessel would need to be competent and strong, to handle the challenges and rigours of leading the Church once He had ascended back to heaven.

Satan, therefore, had been permitted to be an important tool in the sifting and strengthening process that Peter himself, would need to personally navigate. He was not to be wrapped in cotton wool, and protected, but rather fully exposed to Satan, for personal testing and the proving of his core faith and commitment.

This is not the first time we have seen Satan's role, as one of testing and challenging an individual's faith and commitment to God.

The book of Job is devoted to detailing the whole process of Satan's role, in the testing and challenging of Job's commitment to God.

So how does this testing and proving process apply to us?

How does this process enable us to grow and mature in Christ?

If we truly desire to grow in Christ and increasingly reflect His love and life, then we should expect, and even welcome those testing and challenging situations that confront us from time to time, from whoever and from wherever they originate.

> As it was with Peter, it is the reinforcing and strengthening of our faith that is really at stake for "without faith, it's impossible to please God." (Hebrews 11:6)

What we do know is that Peter ultimately denied that he ever knew Christ, and he made that denial, three times, however, that was never the core objective of the sifting process.

What was important was the status and resilience of his spiritual life, his faith, his commitment, and his loyalty to Jesus. These were the things, which were the key focus of this testing process.

Similarly in Job's case, despite the most incredible challenges, tests, and trials, Job's faith stood firm in the face of it all and he declared:

> "Though He slay me, yet will I trust Him" (Job 13:15)

Something else that is important here, is the phrase Jesus used when telling him of Peter's forthcoming testing.

He said, "… when you're converted…."

The Greek word for "converted" is "epistrephō" meaning to 'turn back towards".

This seems to be exactly what happened, in John 21:15-17, when Peter and the resurrected Jesus, met again by the sea of Tiberias.

Despite him being very aware of his denial of Jesus, his core faith and commitment to Christ, were still clearly strong and intact.

Peter may have failed at the human level, but he had not failed at the heart level.

He had not turned back, even though, he would have certainly felt that he had failed Jesus.

Here, at the sea of Tiberias, he renews his relationship with the resurrected Christ and demonstrates that he was ready, not only to be restored in fellowship with Him but also ready to lead the Church following Pentecost.

Jesus affirms once again, that leadership role for him when he says, "…strengthen your brethren".

So, how does this testing and proving process apply to us?

Is there a clearly defined "sifting" process that enables us to mature and grow in Christ?

James highlights that process, like this:

> "My brethren, count it all joy when you fall into various trials, knowing that the testing of your faith produces patience. But let patience have its perfect work, that you may be perfect and complete, lacking nothing." (James 1:2-4)

Peter adds to James' perspective:

> "……though now for a little while, if need be, you have been grieved by various trials, that the genuineness of your faith, being much more precious than gold that perishes, though it is tested by fire, may be found to praise, honour, and glory at the revelation of Jesus Christ" (1 Peter 1:5-7)

Like James and Peter, we should expect these tests and trials, and completely embrace them, because they are designed by God, to serve the purpose of God.

They are intended for our maturing, our strengthening, and our overall spiritual resilience.

> "For this reason, we do not lose heart: Even though our outward man is perishing, yet our inward man is being renewed day by day. Our light affliction, which lasts but for a moment, works for us a far

more exceeding and eternal weight of glory, while we do not look at the things which are seen, but at the things which are not seen." (2 Corinthians 4:16-18)

## CHAPTER THIRTY-EIGHT

# Stephen's Trial by Stoning

**W**hen the number of early Christians in Jerusalem significantly increased, there was, initially, a considerable amount of confusion and a lot of complaining, about the overall support of the poor and, how welfare was distributed to those believers, who were in material need.

> "Now in those days, as the disciples were multiplied, there was murmuring among the Hellenists against the Hebrews, because their widows were overlooked in the daily distribution" (Acts 6:1)

Stephen was one of those early Christians, whose trustworthy character and spiritual prowess caused him to stand out, and so, he was chosen by the Apostles, as one of seven deacons, appointed to organise and then, take care of the welfare and charity activities.

It is worth noting here, that Stephen is a Greek name, Stephanos, and because the appointment of the seven deacons was mainly in response to complaints from Greek-speaking Jewish Christians, it is generally thought that Stephen was also chosen, because he was, himself, a Greek-speaking, Hellenist Jew.

As well as being of a trustworthy character, Stephen, was also a Spirit-filled Christian believer:

> "Stephen...... was a man full of faith and the Holy Spirit... "(Acts 6:5)

He was also a powerful minister in the early Church, and his ministry made a significant impact in Jerusalem:

"Now Stephen, .... did great wonders and miracles among the people…" (Acts 6:5)

However, his ministry was so effective, that many Jews in the city, became extremely anxious about his influence and success:

"Then some men rose up from what is called the Synagogue of the Freedmen (Cyrenians, Alexandrians, and those from Cilicia and of Asia), disputing with Stephen. But they were not able to withstand the wisdom and the Spirit by which he spoke." (Acts 6: 9-10)

These same Jews, retaliated against Stephen, falsely accusing him of blasphemy, and forcing him to stand trial before the Sanhedrin, the Jewish supreme council, at the time:

"Then they secretly instigated men who said, "We have heard him speak blasphemous words against Moses and God." So, they stirred up the people and the elders and the scribes and came upon him and seized him and led him to the Sanhedrin and set up false witnesses". (Acts 6: 12-13)

In front of the Sanhedrin, Stephen powerfully recounted the many past blessings that God had provided for the children of Israel, and the ungrateful and rebellious way, in which they had disobeyed Him. Stephen, then directly accused them of murdering Jesus, whose coming as the promised Messiah, he said, had been foretold by Moses:

"When they heard these things, they were cut to the heart, and they gnashed their teeth at him" (Acts 7: 54)

Stephen, undeterred, continued speaking, and filled with the Holy Spirit, declared that, at that moment, in a vision, he saw the glory of God, and Jesus standing at the right hand of God:

"Look! I see the heavens opened and the Son of Man standing at the right hand of God." (Acts 7:56)

This declaration, outraged them so much, that they turned on Stephen, viciously dragging him outside of the city, where they proceeded to stone him to death:

> "Then they cried out with a loud voice, closed their ears, and rushed at him in unison. And they threw him out of the city and stoned him" (Acts 7:57)

Even in death, though, Stephen remained full of the Holy Spirit and the love of Christ.

Almost identically to Jesus, he declared, as he was battered by the rocks:

> "Lord, do not hold this sin against them." (Acts 7:60)

Stephen's terrible death, though, had the unexpected consequence of forcing Christians to flee the increasing persecution in Jerusalem. This meant though, that the Gospel message, was also taken with them, and, as a result, that message was spread successfully, far beyond Jerusalem.

It is believed that Stephen's death took place in AD 34, not long after Christ's ascension.

His arrest, trial, and martyrdom were also witnessed and approved of, by a young Jewish zealot, whose name was Saul.

This same young man would later turn to Christ and become Paul the Apostle.

## CHAPTER THIRTY-NINE

# Empowered Believers

The Day of Pentecost was a truly momentous day for the Church of Jesus Christ.

It was on that day, that the first Christian believers were filled with the Holy Spirit and became the first empowered members of the Body of Christ. From that point on, and certainly throughout the book of the Acts, we see early Christian believers enthusiastically spreading the Gospel, and also advocating two important baptisms, as an integral part of their message.

These two baptisms were very prominent in the early Church, as they both carried a very strong, and very public expression of an individual's faith in and commitment to Christ.

Firstly, water baptism, where believers, openly, demonstrated their faith in Christ, and particularly, marked a complete separation, from their previously sinful and godless lives.

Paul describes that first baptism:

> "Do you not know that we who were baptized into Jesus Christ were baptized into His death? Therefore, we were buried with Him by baptism into death, that just as Christ was raised up from the dead by the glory of the Father, even so we also should walk in newness of life" (Romans 6:3-4)

The second baptism, the baptism in the Holy Spirit, is one, where believers become empowered to not only, proclaim the full Gospel of Christ, but also minister spiritually to their fellow believers, in the Body of Christ.

Before his ascension back to heaven, Jesus had instructed His disciples that they must wait in Jerusalem. This, He said, was a vitally important step, in their preparation to proclaim, the full Gospel.

He told them:

> "Do not depart from Jerusalem, but wait for the promise of the Father, of which you have heard from Me. For John baptized with water, but you shall be baptized with the Holy Spirit not many days from now." (Acts 1:4-5)

He also explained precisely why they should wait:

> "But you shall receive power when the Holy Spirit comes upon you. And you shall be My witnesses in Jerusalem, and in all Judea and Samaria, and to the ends of the earth." (Acts 1:8)

Throughout the Acts, we see how those same disciples, now empowered apostles, preached, and demonstrated the full Gospel, firstly to the Jews in Jerusalem, and then beyond to the Gentiles. Empowerment meant that the disciples who, up to Pentecost, had been simply disciples of Christ, had now become empowered apostles.

This step of empowerment, clearly fulfilled what Jesus had already prophesied, would happen, following His ascension back to heaven:

> "Truly, truly I say to you, he who believes in Me will do the works that I do also. And he will do greater works than these because I am going to My Father" (John 14:12)

They were firstly, His eyewitnesses, and then, His empowered emissaries, who were now being sent out into the world, to deliver the full Gospel message. Their empowered Gospel message was clear and powerful and is recorded in detail throughout the book of Acts.

Here is one of the more comprehensive examples, of how that Gospel message was delivered, and demonstrated, by the empowered apostles:

> "Many signs and wonders were performed among the people by the hands of the apostles. And they

were all together in Solomon's Porch. No one else dared join them, but the people respected them. Believers were increasingly added to the Lord, crowds of both men and women, so that they even brought the sick out into the streets and placed them on beds and mats, so that at least the shadow of Peter passing by might touch some of them. Crowds also came out of the cities surrounding Jerusalem, bringing the sick and those who were afflicted by evil spirits, and they were all healed." (Acts 5:14-15)

This is the true Gospel of Christ, that they were commanded by Christ, and empowered by the Holy Spirit, to deliver to the world. That commandment of Christ, and the ensuing empowerment by the Holy Spirit, has never been rescinded, we are, as members of the current operational Body of Christ, charged and empowered, to deliver that same Gospel message, to this current world.

That living Gospel is designed, to be delivered in precisely the same manner, as it was two thousand years ago because the resurrected Christ has never changed from that day to this.

"Jesus Christ is the same yesterday, and today, and forever" (Hebrew 13:8)

"For I am the Lord, I do not change" (Malachi 3:6)

The Gospel of Christ is designed not just to be preached but also demonstrated.

First, preached, as Paul explains:

"How then shall they call on Him in whom they have not believed? And how shall they believe in Him of whom they have not heard? And how shall they hear without a preacher? And how shall they preach unless they are sent? As it is written: "How beautiful are the feet of those who preach the Gospel of peace, who bring good news of good things!" (Romans 10:14-15)

However, also demonstrated, as we saw earlier, described by Jesus:

> "Truly, truly I say to you, he who believes in Me will do the works that I do also. And he will do greater works than these because I am going to My Father". (John 14:12)

So, what were those 'works' that Jesus spoke of?
He explains, what those works are, before His Ascension:

> "These signs will accompany those who believe: In My name, they will cast out demons; they will speak with new tongues; they will take up serpents; if they drink any deadly thing, it will not hurt them; they will lay hands on the sick, and they will recover." (Mark 16:17-18)

Peter also reflects on Christ's own Gospel message, delivered during His earthly ministry:

> "......God anointed Jesus of Nazareth with the Holy Spirit and with power, who went about doing good and healing all who were oppressed by the devil, for God was with Him". (Acts 10:38)

We, too, are both commanded and empowered, to deliver the complete Gospel of Christ.

The Great Commission is still in force, and that commandment of Christ has never been retracted.

The essential empowerment of the Holy Spirit is still available, as a gift, for every believer.

Jesus' words still live:

> "But you shall receive power when the Holy Spirit comes upon you. And you shall be My witnesses in Jerusalem, and in all Judea and Samaria, and to the ends of the earth." (Acts 1:8)

## CHAPTER FORTY

# Spiritual Warfare (Part One)

We saw in the previous chapter, that one of the outcomes of the empowerment of the first apostles was evidenced by their ability, among other things, to 'cast out demons'.

We also saw that a key part of Jesus' ministry was:

> "… healing all who were oppressed by the devil, for God was with Him." (Acts 10:38)

From the beginning of time, spiritual conflict has existed between God, the Creator of all things, and Satan, the fallen archangel thrown out of heaven, for his attempt to elevate himself above God. From the Garden of Eden through to Jesus' arrival, there are clear examples of where that conflict and enmity, have repeatedly surfaced.

Jesus Himself highlighted that enmity when He said:

> "…. I will build my church, and the gates of Hell will not overcome it." (Matthew 16:18)

That enmity is particularly evidenced in situations, where mankind is in a healthy and harmonious relationship with God.

The Garden of Eden is the perfect example, of that harmony and relationship. It's where we first see this enmity surface when Eve is tempted by Satan; Adam, is then seduced to sin, and the result is a spiritual catastrophe, for them and for everybody that follows afterward.

Note carefully though, what God says to Satan, following the tragic events in Eden:

> "I will put enmity between you and the woman,
> and between your offspring and her offspring and
> he will bruise your head, and you will bruise his
> heel." (Genesis 3:15).

As a result, and from that point, mankind has been at the centre of this ongoing conflict between God and His Creation and Satan and his cohorts. Equally, Satan's sole objective from that point has been to subvert, spoil, and destroy the fulfillment of the will and purpose of God. Anything and anyone that is chosen by God, and is committed to His will and purpose, becomes a clear target for satanic attacks.

We see this conflict arise again, when God commends Job to Satan, as an example of a righteous and blameless man.

God says to Satan:

> "Have you considered My servant Job, that there
> is none like him on the earth, a blameless and an
> upright man, who fears God, and avoids evil?"
> (Job1:8)

Satan, eager to prove God wrong, responds by saying that Job is only righteous and loyal, because He has prospered him greatly, and protected him and his family, with an impenetrable hedge:

Satan continues and says:

> "But stretch out Your hand now, and touch all that
> he has, and he will curse You to Your face." (Job
> 1:11).

God, amazingly, allows Satan to do his worst, and attack Job, most destructively. What follows is a series of terrible events, which destroys everything that Job has, and tests his commitment and loyalty to God, in the most extreme fashion. However, Job, ultimately survives, by demonstrating his deep and immovable commitment to God, and amid his terrible trials and tribulations, God, rescues, and delivers Him.

Here is what Job says that demonstrates his incredible loyalty and commitment to God, in the face of his terrible troubles:

> "Though he slays me, yet will I trust in him: but

I will maintain mine own ways before him" (Job 13:15)

Our third example is Jesus himself, who, following his baptism by John, was taken by the Holy Spirit into the wilderness where He fasted for forty days and was also tested by Satan. We should remember here that Jesus is the Son of God, but that he has also taken on human form, with all its potential constraints and weaknesses.

Satan knows that Jesus, in his human form has the potential to fail. He then vigorously challenges Jesus three times and tempts him with very specific aspects of his humanity. On each occasion, Jesus responds strongly and positively, by using the Word of God, to repulse and repel Satan.

Each time He responds by saying, "It is written…."

He uses the Word of God and his obedience to it, to overcome Satan. Notice, that it is the very same Word of God, that Adam and Eve disobeyed and subsequently lost their relationship with God.

Jesus uses that same Word, this time to repel and overcome Satan's deceit and trickery. Jesus' responses were, in fact, a glorious payback for Adam's failure in the Garden.

So, how does this conflict between the plan and purpose of God and Satan's attempts to subvert and obstruct those plans, affect us today?

We are, as the church of Jesus Christ, a prime target for Satan's onslaught, just like Adam, Job, and Jesus, Himself. We represent the will and purpose of God, here on Earth.

Peter therefore admonishes us:

> "Be sober and watchful, because your adversary the devil walks around as a roaring lion, seeking whom he may devour. (1 Peter 5:8).

Paul, also affirms the nature of who, and what, we are fighting:

> "For our fight is not against flesh and blood, but against principalities, against powers, against the rulers of the darkness of this world, and spiritual forces of evil in the heavenly places." (Ephesians 6:12)

They are not saying these things to make us fearful, anxious, or alarmed.

Peter's point is that we are to be aware, and alert and to take this conflict seriously. Paul's point is that we are not fighting human-level warfare, but we are fighting spiritual powers, against which we need to be equipped with spiritual armaments and weaponry.

Paul then goes on to underline the determination, with which Satan, will attempt to subvert, and seduce the people of God:

> "For such are false apostles and deceitful workers, disguising themselves as apostles of Christ. And no wonder! For even Satan disguises himself as an angel of light" (2 Corinthians 11:13-14).

So, how do we move forward?

We need to be aware and alert but also, we need to be prepared to stand firm in the victory that Christ has already accomplished on our behalf.

Paul affirms that victory:

> "But thanks be to God, who gives us the victory through our Lord Jesus Christ!" (1 Corinthians 15:57)

He repeats this truth when writing to the Corinthians, for a second time:

> "Now thanks be to God who always causes us to triumph in Christ and through us reveals the fragrance of His knowledge in every place" (2 Corinthians 2:14)

We can and should respond to Satan's deceit and trickery, by doing precisely what Jesus did, by declaring and standing on His Word and promises.

James describes it this way:

> "Therefore, submit yourselves to God. Resist the devil, and he will flee from you." (James 4:7)

So, let us fully embrace those resources, that Christ has provided for us, and go forward, in that victory that He has already accomplished for us, and we will overcome.

> "Therefore, take up the whole armour of God that you may be able to resist in the evil day, and having done all, to stand" (Ephesians 6:13)

## CHAPTER FORTY-ONE

# Spiritual Warfare (Part Two)

In Part One we introduced the spiritual warfare environment, in which we as Christian believers, live.

We were reminded by Peter, who exhorted us to:

> "Be sober and watchful, because your adversary the devil walks around as a roaring lion, seeking whom he may devour. (1 Peter 5:8)

We stressed that he is not saying these things to make us fearful, anxious, or alarmed but that we should be aware, alert, and take this spiritual conflict seriously, we can however, also be positive and full of faith, because Christ has overcome Satan, and in Him, we are already completely victorious.

Victory over Satan and all his evil works have already been achieved by Jesus, and that victory has been handed to the Church, as a gift.

Paul writes:

> "But thanks be to God, who gives us the victory through our Lord Jesus Christ!" (1 Corinthians 15:5)

In Part Two, we will look at additional resources that we can access, that are important weapons in our spiritual armoury, that also need to be utilised in this spiritual conflict. We need to understand, that if we want to experience the victory that Christ has achieved for us, then we have to use all of the resources, the Holy Spirit provides.

Paul reminds us, why this is so:

> "For though we walk in the flesh, we do not war according to the flesh. For the weapons of our warfare are not carnal, but mighty through God to the pulling down of strongholds" (2 Corinthians 10:4)

Paul wants us as individuals and the Church as a whole, to be prepared, skilful, and confident, just as he is:

> "So, therefore, I run, not with uncertainty. So, I fight, not as one who beats the air" (1 Corinthians 9:26)

A major weapon, we already highlighted in Part One, is the Word of God. We know that Jesus repulsed Satan's efforts in the wilderness, by declaring "It is written….", three times. He stood on God's Word and silenced Satan, He showed that the forces of Satan, cannot withstand the power and authority of God's Word.

Isaiah states:

> "For as the rain comes down, and the snow from heaven, and do not return there but water the earth and make it bring forth and bud that it may give seed to the Sower and bread to the eater, so shall My word be that goes forth from My mouth; it shall not return to Me void, but it shall accomplish that which I please, and it shall prosper in the thing for which I sent it." (Isaiah 55:11).

Jeremiah reinforces the power and might of the Word of God:

> "Is not My word like fire, says the Lord, and like a hammer that breaks the rock in pieces?" (Jeremiah 23:29)

We have other resources too, which we need to use in this spiritual conflict.

Paul introduces some of those resources, when describing his ministerial credentials, to the Corinthian church.

He says:

"By the word of truth, by the power of God, by the
armour of righteousness on the right hand and the
left..." (2 Corinthians 6:7)

He elaborates further on the "armour of righteousness", and
why its protection is so very important for each of us, as believers:

"Finally, my brothers, be strong in the Lord and
the power of His might. Put on the whole armour
of God that you may be able to stand against the
schemes of the devil. For our fight is not against
flesh and blood, but against principalities, against
powers, against the rulers of the darkness of this
world, and spiritual forces of evil in the heavenly
places. Therefore, take up the whole armour of God
that you may be able to resist in the evil day, and
having done all, to stand". (Ephesians 6:10-13)

So, what is the whole armour of God?

Paul details each piece of this all-important, spiritual armour,
in Ephesians 6:14-17, and we are instructed to put on, by faith,
each piece.

Paul, begins, with "your waist girded with truth" which means
that we, as individuals and the Church as a whole, are required
to actively embrace and cloth ourselves with the instruction, the
direction, and above all, the truth, that emanates, directly and
exclusively, from the Holy Spirit.

We have stressed, throughout the pages of this book, the absolute necessity to acknowledge and submit to the will and direction
of the Holy Spirit, both as individuals and as the Body of Christ.

Jesus said: "But when the Spirit of truth comes, He will guide
you into all truth" (John 16:13)

Paul points to the incredible power and strength of the truth:

"For we can do nothing against the truth, but only
for the truth" (2 Corinthians 13:8).

"Put on the breastplate of righteousness" directs us to own and
confess, that we do not stand before God or anyone else, in our righteousness, but we stand only in the perfect righteousness of Christ.

We ought to note here, exactly what the breastplate protects.

It is designed specially, to protect the heart and other vital organs.

So, for the believer, it is significant that Paul associates 'righteousness' with the heart.

We know that Satan is described as the 'accuser of the brethren'. (Revelation 12:10)

Satan's strategy is to look for any way he can, to blame, accuse, and condemn us, and make us try to justify ourselves, rather than maintain our focus on the righteousness of Christ.

Where does the ensuing condemnation, then look to reside?

John explains:

> "For if our heart condemns us, God is greater than our heart and knows everything. (1 John 3:20)

So, Paul reaffirms the importance of the breastplate of righteousness, because the heart is the most important, yet also a most vulnerable organ. Not only is it where condemnation seeks to make its home, but it is also the seat of our faith as it is "with the heart that man believes".

So, Paul encourages us:

> "......and be found in Him, not having my righteousness which is from the law, but that which is through faith in Christ, the righteousness which is of God on the basis of faith." (Philippians 3:9)

We must also take a lead, from Jesus, who took great care in signalling where all righteousness, virtue, and goodness are situated when responding to the rich, young ruler:

> "He said to him, "Why do you call Me good? No one is good, except God alone" (Mark 10:18).

"Feet fitted with the readiness of the Gospel of peace" points to our absolute readiness to declare and demonstrate the full Gospel of Christ - at any time, to anyone, anywhere.

It's no coincidence that Isaiah had already, centuries before, highlighted the feet as being of great beauty, in connection with those who proclaim the Gospel:

> "How beautiful upon the mountains are the feet of
> him who brings good news, who proclaims peace,
> who brings good news of happiness, who proclaims
> salvation, who says to Zion, "Your God reigns!"
> (Isaiah 52:7)

Peter also highlights this need for readiness in respect of proclaiming the Gospel:

> "Always be ready to answer every man who asks
> you for a reason for the hope that is in you, with
> gentleness and fear." (1 Peter 3:15)

Jesus' instruction to his disciples also stands true today, and our readiness to share the Gospel of Christ, is part of our spiritual armoury with which we wage war, against the powers of darkness.

> "He said to them, "Go into all the world, and
> preach the gospel to every creature." (Mark 16:15)

Our constant readiness to declare the Gospel is a true representation of the military strategy that is described as "the best form of defence is attack"!

"Take up the shield of faith" is a powerful weapon, we have previously covered in some detail, in Chapters Seventeen and Eighteen.

Faith here again means standing firm upon and protecting ourselves with, the Word of God in the face of anything and everything that Satan might hurl at us.

Interestingly, faith, serves two spiritual purposes, in the armour of God. Faith is an attack weapon but is also a defensive weapon.

Paul exhorts Timothy to "fight the good fight of faith," in other words, to go and attack Satan and his minions, using the shield of faith.

He then exhorts the Ephesians:

> "Above all taking the shield of faith, with which
> you will be able to extinguish all the fiery arrows of
> the evil one" (Ephesians 6:16).

On this occasion though, he says to defend ourselves against Satan's weaponry, using the same shield of faith.

"Take the Helmet of Salvation" focuses on the fact, that we are engaging in this spiritual conflict, as those, who enjoy the saving power of Christ, and as redeemed members of the Church of Jesus Christ.

We also need to recognise, that a helmet, protects the head, and the human brain, which like the heart, is an incredibly important organ of the body.

With this in mind, it is extremely important, to revisit the original meaning of the word, "salvation". We already looked at the true meaning of the Greek word for 'salvation' in Chapter Twenty.

We saw that its original meaning is far more wide-ranging than the English word suggests. That original meaning helps us, enormously to see the significance of the "helmet of salvation," and why it's such a key part of the armour of God.

The Greek word for 'salvation' is 'soterion.'

Its core meaning covers, not only our deliverance from sin and being born again but also our continuing and ongoing preservation and safety. So, salvation, being such an important part of our spiritual armoury, adds even more significance to Paul's exhortation, "work out your own salvation".

The final piece of the armour of God is the 'Sword of the Spirit, which is the Word of God'.

The Word of God is an 'attack' weapon, in the armoury of God.

We saw the function of God's Word, in the previous chapter:

> "Is not My word like fire, says the Lord, and like a hammer that breaks the rock in pieces?" (Jeremiah 23:29)

Jesus wielded God's Word, three times during His wilderness test, and each time, He repelled Satan. He declared, three times, 'It is written…." and each time, He put Satan to flight.

Paul echoes Jeremiah's words:

> "For the word of God is alive, and active, and sharper than any two-edged sword, piercing even to the division of soul and spirit, of joints and marrow, and able to judge the thoughts and intents of the heart." (Hebrews 4:12).

So, let us embrace and utilise, by faith, the spiritual weaponry that God has provided for us as believers and as the Church of Jesus Christ- those weapons that are for defence and those weapons that are for attack.

Let us, as a matter of priority and importance, put on, and keep on, by faith, the complete armour of God.

> "For though we walk in the flesh, we do not war according to the flesh. For the weapons of our warfare are not carnal, but mighty through God to the pulling down of strongholds" (2 Corinthians 10:4)

CHAPTER FORTY-TWO

# The Baptism in the
# Holy Spirit

I n Chapter Thirty-Nine, we introduced the whole principle of Empowered Believers.

In that chapter, we looked at how the disciples, who for three years or so had been simply followers of Christ, were transformed on the day of Pentecost, into empowered apostles, equipped to take the Gospel of Christ out into the world.

Before the Day of Pentecost and after His resurrection, Jesus reconnected with his disciples as they were gathered behind locked doors in a room somewhere in Jerusalem. He showed them the scars on His hands and feet thus proving He was, in fact, Jesus,

He then said to them, "Peace to you! As the Father has sent Me, I also send you." And when He had said this, He breathed on them, and said to them, "Receive the Holy Spirit".

Christ had died and been raised from the dead and so had now become truly the 'Lamb of God that had taken away the sin of the world'.

It was only now, that the disciples could enter into all the benefits of Christ's ultimate sacrifice and embrace their salvation. They would now cease being simply Jesus' disciples, and become spiritually alive apostles, commissioned by Jesus, to declare the Gospel of salvation to the world.

This is the point, at which the disciples, were 'born again of incorruptible seed by the Word of God'.

It is at this point that the Holy Spirit enters them, and they experience what Paul later explained:

'But if the Spirit of Him who raised Jesus from the

dead dwells in you, He who raised Christ from the dead will also give life to your mortal bodies through His Spirit who dwells in you'. (Romans 8:11)

They were the first born-again believers.

However, this was only the first step in their commissioning process. At this point, they were made spiritually alive as a result of Jesus breathing on them, but they still needed to be, spiritually empowered.

Being spiritually alive, was about their salvation, but being spiritually empowered, was about their authority and capability, to preach and demonstrate the power of the Gospel, with the same power that Jesus had possessed, during his earthly ministry.

And so, Jesus, instructs them about their next step which is spiritual empowerment.

> 'And being assembled with them, He commanded them not to depart from Jerusalem, but to wait for the Promise of the Father, "which," He said, "you have heard from Me....but you shall receive power when the Holy Spirit has come upon you, and you shall be witnesses to Me in Jerusalem, and in all Judea and Samaria, and to the end of the earth...... for John truly baptized with water, but you shall be baptized with the Holy Spirit not many days from now." (Acts 1:4-6)

The new believers complied with his instructions and a short time later after his Ascension, we see the words of Jesus, fulfilled:

> "When the Day of Pentecost had fully come, they were all with one accord in one place. And suddenly there came a sound from heaven, as of a rushing mighty wind, and it filled the whole house where they were sitting. Then there appeared to them divided tongues, as of fire, and one sat upon each of them. And they were all filled with the Holy Spirit and began to speak with other tongues, as the Spirit gave them utterance" (Acts 2:1-4)

This then, was the second important phase of Christ's commissioning process, their empowerment to preach the complete Gospel, with authority and confidence.

The evidence of this empowerment is summarised in Acts 5:

> "And through the hands of the apostles, many signs and wonders were done among the people. And they were all with one accord in Solomon's Porch. Yet none of the rest dared join them, but the people esteemed them highly. And believers were increasingly added to the Lord, multitudes of both men and women, so that they brought the sick out into the streets and laid them on beds and couches, that at least the shadow of Peter passing by might fall on some of them. Also, a multitude gathered from the surrounding cities to Jerusalem, bringing sick people and those who were tormented by unclean spirits, and they were all healed."

This empowerment process was not just for the first apostles, residing in Jerusalem. We see other examples, of new believers, being infilled by the Holy Spirit.

In Samaria:

> "Now when the apostles who were at Jerusalem heard that Samaria had received the word of God, they sent Peter and John to them, who, when they had come down, prayed for them that they might receive the Holy Spirit. For as yet He had fallen upon none of them. They had only been baptised in the name of the Lord Jesus" (Acts 8:14-16).

In Ephesus:

> "When they heard this, they were baptized in the name of the Lord Jesus. And when Paul had laid hands on them, the Holy Spirit came upon them, and they spoke with tongues and prophesied" (Acts 19:5)

These important foundation steps are still in place for every believer and not just for those in the early Church. We are invited to embrace Christ as Saviour, and by the power of the Holy Spirit, to be 'born again'. However, we are also invited to be empowered by the same Holy Spirit, to deliver and demonstrate the power of the Gospel to others, with boldness and confidence.

There are a considerable number of believers, who like the believers in Ephesus, have never received the empowerment of the Holy Spirit. Some simply do not know that baptism in the Holy Spirit is available to them.

Others have been misled and told that this experience is no longer available today and there are others, who simply believe, for some reason, that it is not for them. We need to understand that this empowerment by the Holy Spirit, is not just an optional extra.

It's an absolute necessity for every believer so that we can effectively represent Christ, and take our place in the Body of Christ, as ministers of the true Gospel.

So, if you have not been baptised in the Holy Spirit, the question that Paul asked in Ephesus, remains:

> "Have you received the Holy Ghost since you believed?" (Acts 19:2)

## CHAPTER FORTY-THREE

# The Gifts of the Holy Spirit (Part One)

In Chapter Three, 'What is the Body of Christ', we highlighted that the Body of Christ is a spiritual community, of which every baptised, born-again believer, is a part.

The function of the Body of Christ is for each of its members to share and minister to their fellow believers so that they can each grow and mature, into the fullness of Christ. We have been directed by Christ, and empowered by the Holy Spirit, to make a spiritual contribution, to each other's lives.

Paul describes it this way:

> "But the manifestation of the Spirit is given to every man to profit withal". (1 Corinthians 12:7)

He clarifies this point further when writing to the Corinthian church:

> "How is it then, brothers? When you come together, every one of you has a psalm, a teaching, a tongue, a revelation, and an interpretation. Let all things be done for edification." (1 Corinthians 14:26).

To ensure that each of us is properly equipped to deliver support, help, and aid to each other, Paul identifies some unique spiritual tools, which enable us to be highly effective in our ministry, one to another.

1 Corinthians 12, actually opens with Paul, stating clearly that we need, as the Body of Christ, to be informed about these unique spiritual tools and not to be ignorant.

He says:

"Now concerning spiritual gifts, brethren, I do not
want you to be ignorant".

He then takes time to explain, in as much detail as necessary, all
that we need to know to avail ourselves of these heavenly resources.

Paul, then describes these unique, spiritual resources which we
know, as the gifts of the Holy Spirit:

"To one is given by the Spirit the word of wisdom, to another the word of knowledge by the
same Spirit, to another faith by the same Spirit,
to another gifts of healings by the same Spirit, to
another the working of miracles, to another prophecy, to another discerning of spirits, to another various kinds of tongues, and another the interpretation of tongues." (1 Corinthians 12:7-10)

Before we look at each gift in Chapter Forty-Four, we need to
pay attention, to how Paul describes what our attitude and motivation should be, to acquiring and using these gifts of the Spirit.

Paul said this:

"But earnestly covet the greater gifts." (1 Corinthians 12:31)

'Covet' would seem to be an odd word to use, as it is usually
perceived as a negative word, and normally preceded by "Don't!"

The Greek word for 'covet' is 'zeloo'.

It means, among other things, 'to burn with zeal for' or, 'to be
zealous in pursuit'.

By using this particular word, Paul is being very clear about the
importance he is placing on the spiritual gifts, and their application
in the Church of Jesus Christ.

He is also expressing the need for each member, to understand,
just how important, the role of the gifts is, at the personal level. He
is telling the believers at Corinth, to pursue these spiritual gifts,
with great enthusiasm and energy. He wants them, "to be zealous
in the pursuit" of the gifts.

He needs them to understand, that their embracing of the spiritual gifts, is a high priority, and, that these gifts should be seen

as highly important, as they are a crucial part of how the Church builds itself up and how it grows and matures.

The focus here is the edification or the building up of the Church and its members.

He emphasises this factor again, later in the same letter:

> "Even so you, since you are zealous for spiritual gifts, let it be for the edification of the church that you seek to excel". (1 Corinthians 14:12)

He also clarified the same message, in Ephesians 4:15-16:

> ".... speaking the truth in love, (we) may grow up in all things into Him who is the head—Christ— from whom the whole body, joined and knit together by what every joint supplies, according to the effective working by which every part does its share, causes growth of the body for the edifying of itself in love".

The spiritual gifts, he is saying, are a key part of how we share, minister, grow, and edify each other.

So given this degree of clarity, you would think that the role and practice of these self-same spiritual gifts would be very clearly understood and demonstrated across the whole Church.

Unfortunately, the role and application of the spiritual gifts are not taught regularly or demonstrated, in most of our Churches, in fact, they almost appear to be ignored, 'in plain sight', meaning, that they are deliberately overlooked in many, many churches.

In an extreme case, there is a movement described as "Cessationist", which believes these manifestations of the Spirit, were removed by God when the first apostles died.

One of the issues that often leads to a misunderstanding, is the second part of our opening verse:

> "But covet earnestly the best gifts: and yet shew I unto you a more excellent way". (1 Corinthians 12:31)

The misunderstanding is many times exploited by those ministers, who dismiss the importance of spiritual gifts, in today's

Church environment and our gatherings.

Frequently, they will declare that what Paul is stating here, is that there is a "more excellent way", than the use of the gifts of the Spirit.

They then move to Chapter Thirteen and further affirm that the more excellent way is love. They contend, that if you demonstrate the love of God as much and as often as you can, then, that love supersedes any need at all for the gifts of the Spirit because agape love is "the more excellent way".

On the face of it, it appears to be a plausible argument, but on closer attention, it doesn't stand the test of being, in any way, authentic.

So, what is Paul saying here?

The truth is what precedes it in the first part of the verse. "Covet earnestly the best gifts….".

Paul is saying earnestly pursue spiritual gifts, desire them, and seek to use them with great determination.

Why?

Because as we have seen already, the edifying and strengthening of the Church is of vital importance, and, that process of edification, is the prime objective for the use of the gifts of the Spirit.

However, what he is highlighting is, that rather than being motivated to use the gifts by simply "coveting" them, we should seek to be motivated by God's love, when we look to use them.

In Chapter Thirteen, he continues to explain why love is such a more excellent reason for using the gifts of the Spirit, rather than just simply, "coveting" them.

That is the "more excellent way" to which he is referring.

He is saying, "Be motivated by love, but, at the same time, don't ever lose your enthusiasm in pursuing their use".

So, how do we move forward?

What is the Holy Spirit emphasising currently?

There are several areas that the Holy Spirit is focusing upon, and the gifts of the Holy Spirit are one such area.

Each of the gifts of the Holy Spirit laid out by Paul has a key role to play, in both the preaching of the full Gospel to a lost world, and also in the nourishment and edification of the Church itself.

There is no complete Gospel message, without these spiritual gifts being in operation, through Spirit-filled believers. There is no regular nourishment of the Body of Christ either, without the gifts of the Holy Spirit being used regularly, across the Church.

To understate, and subsequently suppress, these incredible manifestations of the Spirit, is to quench and grieve the Holy Spirit.

Any such suppression also deprives the Body of Christ, of so much that Jesus explained and taught the disciples in John, chapters 14-16, about the crucial role and operation of the Holy Spirit once he had ascended.

I believe, that before Christ's return, there will be a full return, to what was experienced by the early Church, and described so well, in the Acts of the Apostles and throughout Paul's letters.

No longer should we be content with a Gospel and Church gatherings that can only be described as delivering "… a form of godliness but denying the power thereof."

So, let us acknowledge and embrace Paul's exhortation and "covet earnestly the best gifts…."

The Gospel needs to be delivered with power and the Church nourished with the finest diet that Heaven can provide.

## CHAPTER FORTY-FOUR

# The Gifts of the Holy Spirit (Part Two)

In Part One, we looked at the overall need to embrace the gifts of the Holy Spirit with energy and commitment and to seek to be motivated to use them, by our love for one another.

Paul summarised it so well when he wrote "Covet earnestly the best gifts: and yet shew I unto you a more excellent way" We saw that agape love will seek to pursue and use the gifts of the Spirit to edify, support, and minister to the Church, to each of its members and beyond.

Paul put it this way:

> "But the manifestation of the Spirit is given to every man to profit withal". (1 Corinthians 12:7)

One important thing to think about is that the various gifts of the Spirit represent Christ's ministry, and how that ministry is then manifested, through and across the Church.

Before we review the first four gifts individually, let us remind ourselves of one very important thing.

The gifts are "of the Spirit". They are not enhanced human characteristics or human capabilities, that somehow, turn us into 'super-human' people.

The gifts are pure manifestations of the Holy Spirit flowing through us, as members of His Body, and out into the Church, in various forms of spiritual nourishment, direction, and support.

We are channels of the Holy Spirit, and the gifts are manifestations of that Holy Spirit.

As Paul declared:

"But we have this treasure in earthen vessels, that
the excellency of the power may be of God, and not
of us" (2 Corinthians 4:7)

So, let's review 1 Corinthians 12:8-10 and take a look at those
first four gifts.

The first gift of the Spirit is 'Wisdom':

The Greek word here is 'sophia', meaning a higher level of
wisdom, much more related to divine or spiritual wisdom. This
is a demonstration of wisdom or insight, beyond what would be
viewed, as the norm.

A person demonstrating this level of wisdom might be well
defined as extremely learned or demonstrating extreme mastery
when imparting Christian truth.

As we shall see, a person demonstrating this gift of wisdom
may not necessarily be perceived as being wise by normal human
standards.

This level of wisdom is divine and supernatural and has been
made available to the Body of Christ, by the Holy Spirit.

Paul states, that this is made possible, because, in the Head of
the Body, Christ:

"...... are hid all the treasures of wisdom and
knowledge" (Colossians 2:2)

Solomon is renowned as being the wisest king of Israel, ever.

He prayed to God for wisdom, and God honoured him with,
not only wisdom but also riches and honour:

"I have given thee a wise and an understanding
heart; so that there was none like thee before thee,
neither after thee shall any arise like unto thee. And
I have also given thee that which thou hast not
asked, both riches and honour" (1 Kings 3:12-14).

Solomon is also acknowledged as being the author of a large
part of the book of Proverbs, credited, as being the source of some
of the greatest wisdom, known to mankind.

There are also examples of this extraordinary wisdom and
insight in the New Testament.

Firstly, exhibited by Jesus, and recorded by John:

> "Then the Jews were perplexed. They said, "How
> did this man (Jesus) become learned and so versed
> in the Scriptures and theology without formal
> training?" (John 7:15)

Stephen, the first martyr, also demonstrated extraordinary wisdom, as an early member and prominent minister, in the early Church:

> "Then there arose certain of the synagogue, which
> is called the synagogue of the Libertines, and Cyre-
> nians, and Alexandrians, and of them of Cilicia and
> Asia, disputing with Stephen. And they were not
> able to resist the wisdom and the spirit by which he
> spake" (Acts 6:10)

We also know how Peter and John's abilities and skills were viewed by the religious leaders of the day:

> "Now when they saw the boldness of Peter and
> John, and perceived that they were unlearned
> and ignorant men, they marvelled, and they took
> knowledge of them, that they had been with Jesus"
> (Acts 4:13).

This wisdom is so important to the church, that Paul prays specifically for the Spirit of wisdom and revelation:

> "……. that the God of our Lord Jesus Christ, the
> Father of glory, may give you the Spirit of wisdom
> and revelation in the knowledge of Him" (Ephe-
> sians 1:17)

'Knowledge' is the next gift of the Spirit which Paul highlights.

Again, this gift of the Spirit, relates to a much higher level of knowledge, than one could possess through normal means. This form of knowledge relates primarily to an inspired piece of oth-erwise, unknown, information, delivered to an individual, by the Holy Spirit.

Jesus demonstrated this kind of knowledge when talking with

the woman taken in adultery:

> "The woman answered and said, I have no hus-
> band. Jesus said unto her, thou hast well said, I
> have no husband. For thou hast had five husbands,
> and he whom thou now hast is not thy husband: in
> that saidst thou truly". (John 4:17-18).

Jesus, also accessed divine knowledge about Nathaniel:

> "Nathaniel said to Him, "How do You know me?"
> Jesus answered him, "Before Philip called you,
> when you were under the fig tree, I saw you." (John
> 1:48)

Peter also demonstrated previously unknown knowledge when confronting Ananias and Sapphira for lying to the Holy Spirit:

> "But Peter said, Ananias, why hath Satan filled
> thine heart to lie to the Holy Ghost, and to keep
> back part of the price of the land?" (Acts 5:3).

In none of these examples, was the information known before-hand, but was revealed to Jesus and Peter by the Holy Spirit.

Paul moves on to the third gift of the Spirit, 'Faith'.

We need to remember that this is faith, as a manifestation of the Holy Spirit.

This is an extraordinary divine gift of faith, energised by the Holy Spirit, and capable of producing an extraordinary outcome.

Peter demonstrated extraordinary faith, when confronted by the crippled man, begging at the gate of the Temple:

> "I have no silver and gold, but I give you what I
> have. In the name of Jesus Christ of Nazareth, rise
> and walk." (Acts 3:6)

This same level of faith was also displayed by Stephen, in the early stages of the Church's formation in Jerusalem:

> "And Stephen, full of faith and power, did great
> wonders and miracles among the peoples". (Acts
> 6:8)

Paul certainly demonstrated this extraordinary faith, when he and his fellow passengers were confronted with almost certain death, in the face of a raging storm:

> "Wherefore, sirs, be of good cheer: for I believe God, that it shall be even as it had told me…. And so it came to pass, that they escaped all safe to land." (Acts 27:25,44)

The next gift of the Spirit that Paul describes is 'the Gifts of Healing'.

The gifts of healing, again, are represented as extraordinary healing of otherwise, incurable sicknesses, diseases, and physical conditions.

Notice, that it's, translated as "gifts" in the plural, which suggests that healing, can be provided by the Holy Spirit, for more than just physical needs. The gifts of healing, then, cover those, who are mentally, emotionally, and physiologically sick.

There are many, many examples of the gift of healing in the early Church especially.

Peter's very shadow, brought about supernatural healing:

> "…so that they brought the sick out into the streets and laid them on beds and couches, that at least the shadow of Peter passing by might fall on some of them. (Acts 5:15)

Paul exercised the gift of healing:

> "It happened that the father of Publius lay sick with a fever and dysentery. Paul visited him and placing his hands on him, prayed and healed him." (Acts 28:8)

Following this miracle of healing, the word spread across the island of Malta:

> "When this happened, the rest on the island who had diseases also came and were healed." (Acts 28:9)

God has provided incredible power and authority to the church, via these incredible gifts of the Holy Spirit. As believers, we need to be very clear and very confident and embrace Paul's exhortation:

> "Covet earnestly the best gifts". (1 Corinthians 12:31)

Which of the gifts we have covered so far, resonate with you?

In what way is the Holy Spirit moving you, as far as the gifts of the Spirit are concerned?

Using the measure of faith that we all have received, reach out to the Lord, and receive from him, the gifts you genuinely desire, however, above all, be stimulated by the love of God to give, share, and minister the blessing that these gifts provide.

In the next chapter, we will review the remaining five gifts of the Holy Spirit.

## CHAPTER FORTY-FIVE

# The Gifts of the Holy Spirit (Part Three)

In Part One, we looked at why the Church must embrace the gifts of the Spirit with enthusiasm and energy.

In Part Two, we reviewed the first four gifts that Paul listed in 1 Corinthians 12:8-10: Wisdom, the Word of Knowledge, Faith, and Healing.

In Part Three, we will review the remaining five gifts of the Spirit.

They are the Working of Miracles, Prophecy, the Discerning of Spirits, Different Kinds of Tongues, and the Interpretation of Tongues.

Let us start with the Working of Miracles.

We will define 'miracles' as proven, supernatural events, which defy any logical or scientific explanation.

Job declares that supernatural acts and wonders are typical of the nature of God Himself:

> "Indeed, I would appeal to God, and before God, I would set forth my case, who does the great and the inscrutable, wonders without number." (Job 5:8-9)

Miracles are recorded fairly regularly, throughout the Scriptures.

In the Old Testament, we see well-known examples of supernatural events, like the opening of the Red Sea, the fall of the walls of Jericho, and the three Hebrew men, surviving Nebuchadnezzar's fiery furnace.

The very creation of the world in which we live, was probably the most incredible series of miracles, to have ever taken place.

Miracles also occurred regularly throughout the New Testament as well.

They are recorded in the Gospels, covering Jesus' earthly ministry, and in the Acts of the Apostles which covered the history of the early Church.

Two miracles of Jesus, which are probably among the best known, are when He turned the water into wine, recorded by John, and the calming of the raging storm, recorded by Mark.

Christ's resurrection from the dead, which sealed our salvation, is probably one of the most incredible miracles, recorded in the whole of the New Testament.

There are numerous instances recorded of miracles being performed in the early Church:

> "And Stephen, full of faith and power, did great wonders and miracles among the people" (Acts 6:8)

> "And God wrought special miracles by the hands of Paul: so that from his body were brought unto the sick handkerchiefs or aprons, and the diseases departed from them, and the evil spirits went out of them" (Acts 19:11-12)

In these last days, we should not be at all surprised, as we see an increase in the gift of miracles, being seen in action in, and through, the Church.

The next gift of the Spirit that Paul highlights is Prophecy.

Prophecy is, again, a commonplace occurrence throughout the Scriptures, especially in the Old Testament. There is even a complete section of the Old Testament, which is categorized as, 'The Prophets.'

Paul affirms the role of the Old Testament prophets, as the mouthpieces of God, Himself:

> "God, who at various times and in diverse ways spoke long ago to the fathers through the prophets…" (Hebrews 1:1)

Amos, himself a prophet of God, declares:

> "Surely the Lord God does nothing without

revealing His purpose to His servants the prophets." (Amos 3:7)

Even Jesus' ministry, was heralded by prophetic words, from
John the Baptist:

> "And you, child, will be called the prophet of the
> Highest; for you will go before the face of the Lord
> to prepare His ways" (John 1:76)

So, we can see that Prophecy has two specific perspectives.

Amos highlights one perspective which is delivering God's
word regarding some future event or, as Paul highlights, presenting
God's word and direction about a current situation.

So, to what extent did prophecy, occur in the early Church?

The gift of prophecy was evident and regularly demonstrated
on a widespread basis, across the Church.

We know that Peter declared on the day of Pentecost, that the
outpouring of the Holy Spirit, which they had just experienced,
was a fulfillment of Joel's prophecy:

> "And it shall come to pass afterward that I will pour
> out my Spirit upon all flesh, and your sons and
> daughters shall prophesy...." (Acts 2:17)

We can also see, within Joel's prophecy, that 'your sons and
daughters shall prophesy'.

Prophecy, therefore, was always intended to be a direct outcome of the Holy Spirit being poured out on the Church.

The gift of prophecy was also clearly apparent when the believers in Ephesus were also filled with the Holy Spirit:

> "And when Paul had laid hands on them, the
> Holy Spirit came upon them, and they spoke with
> tongues and prophesied." (Acts 19:6)

A man named Agabus also prophesied, this time about a future
event:

> "One of them, named Agabus, stood up and
> prophesied by the Spirit that there would be a great

famine throughout all the world, which came to pass in the days of Claudius Caesar" (Acts 11:28)

Paul makes, what almost appears to be a passing comment, about Philip's daughters:

"….and entered the house of Philip the evangelist, who was one of the seven, and stayed with him. Now this man had four virgin daughters who prophesied". (Acts 21:9)

Paul also highlights the role of prophecy when he encourages Timothy:

"Do not neglect the gift that was given you by prophecy when the council of elders laid their hands upon you" (1 Timothy 4:14)

Paul encourages the Corinthian church:

"Pursue love, and desire spiritual gifts, but especially that you may prophesy". (1 Corinthians 14:1)

Paul then goes on to highlight why prophecy is so important in the Church:

"He that prophesied speaketh unto men to edification, exhortation and comfort" (1 Corinthians 14:3)

Of all the spiritual gifts, Paul is clearly directing the Body of Christ to recognise and elevate the importance of the gift of prophecy:

"For you may all prophesy one by one, that all may learn, and all may be encouraged." (1 Corinthians 14:31).

See how Paul, again, highlights the spiritual value of prophecy, in the Church – learning and encouragement for everybody.

This elevated level of importance indicated by Paul, and also the widespread nature of prophecy across the early Church, shows just how crucial the gift of prophecy, was to the Church, then and still has to be, in today's Church as well.

Prophecy declares the "here and now" nature of the Holy Spirit's voice, speaking His will and purpose into important situations and giving specific direction to individuals and whole church communities.

Let us look next at the gift of the Discerning of Spirits.

Let us clarify first, the focus of this particular gift.

The Greek word for 'discerning' is 'diakrisis' which means either 'a judgment' or 'a diagnosis'. The word has a particular focus in that, it either judges or diagnoses, that which is genuine, as opposed to that which is a counterfeit.

We should note that there is also a more general level of spiritual discernment, which comes with our overall maturity as a Christian believer.

Paul highlights the development of personal discernment, as we each mature spiritually:

> "But solid food belongs to those who are of full age, that is, those who because of use have their senses exercised to discern both good and evil". (Hebrews 5:14)

The gift of discerning of spirits, though, is different in its focus, and with its own clearly defined role, in the Church. This gift provides the Church with the ability to distinguish between the truth coming from the Holy Spirit, and the deceptive doctrines, propagated by men, and even by demons.

Peter, highlights the threat of deceptive doctrines and false teaching:

> "But there were false prophets also among the people, even as there shall be false teachers among you, who privily shall bring in damnable heresies, even denying the Lord that bought them and bring upon themselves swift destruction" (2 Peter 2:1)

Paul, similarly, warns the church at Colossae:

> "Beware lest anyone captivate you through philosophy and vain deceit, in the tradition of men and

the elementary principles of the world, and not after Christ" (Colossians 2:8)

Paul, also alerts the Corinthians:

"For such are false apostles, deceitful workers, transforming themselves into the apostles of Christ. And no marvel; for Satan himself is transformed into an angel of light" (2 Corinthians 11: 13-14).

Paul again:

"But even Titus, who was with me, though he was a Greek, was not compelled to be circumcised. This happened because false brothers were secretly brought in, who sneaked in to spy out our liberty, which we have in Christ Jesus, that they might bring us into bondage." (Galatians 2:4)

Paul demonstrated the gift of discerning of spirits when he called out Elymas:

"O full of all deceit and all fraud, you son of the devil, you enemy of all righteousness, will you not cease perverting the straight ways of the Lord?" (Acts 13:10).

So, do we need to embrace the gift of discerning of spirits in the Church today?

We most certainly do!

With multiple denominations, an incredible variety of Bible translations, and countless ministers and ministries, there is absolutely a continuing need, for the gift of the discerning of spirits.

Like spiritual radar, this gift is vitally important and needs to be continuously operating, in every gathering of the Body of Christ, so that we are continuously absorbing the truth, and not embracing the deception of men, and even demons.

We will conclude our overview of the gifts of the Holy Spirit, by reviewing the gifts of tongues and the interpretation of tongues. It is helpful to cover them together, as their connection is obvious.

The gift of tongues is the gift of speaking fluently in a language, which is unknown to the speaker. The gift of interpretation of tongues is, therefore, the gift of interpreting any message or utterance, that has been delivered in an unknown tongue.

The Greek word for tongues is 'glossa' which means a language, but also clarifies that it is a language that's unknown to the speaker.

Jesus spoke of this particular gift:

> "And these signs will follow those who believe: In My name, they will cast out demons; they will speak with new tongues". (Mark 16:17)

The very first manifestation of the gift of tongues was seen in the Upper Room, on the Day of Pentecost:

> "And they were all filled with the Holy Spirit and began to speak with other tongues, as the Spirit gave them utterance". (Acts 2:4)

This ability to speak in other languages was also manifested by Peter and the others, in Jerusalem, on the same day:

> "And there were dwelling in Jerusalem Jews, devout men, from every nation under heaven. And when this sound occurred, the multitude came together, and were confused, because everyone heard them speak in his own language". (Acts 2:5-6)

On this occasion, there was no need for the gift of interpretation, as everyone heard the message delivered in their language:

> "Then they were all amazed and marvelled, saying to one another, "Look, are not all these who speak Galileans? And how is it that we hear, each in our own language in which we were born?" (Acts 2:7)

The gift of speaking in tongues was also evidence of being baptised in the Holy Spirit, even after Pentecost:

> "And those of the circumcision who believed were astonished, as many as came with Peter, because the gift of the Holy Spirit had been poured out on

the Gentiles also. For they heard them speak with tongues and magnify God". (Acts 10:46)

"And when Paul had laid hands on them, the Holy Spirit came upon them, and they spoke with tongues and prophesied". (Acts 19:6)

So, in what circumstances does the gift of interpretation come into action?

Paul explains:

"Even so you, since you are zealous for spiritual gifts, let it be for the edification of the church that you seek to excel. Therefore, let him who speaks in a tongue pray that he may interpret". (1 Corinthians 14:12-13)

Why? Because other than the Day of Pentecost, speaking in other tongues, almost always requires an interpretation, otherwise there is no obvious purpose.

Why would the Holy Spirit, ever deliver a message in an unknown tongue, which no one can understand?

Paul confirms the consequences of tongues without an interpretation:

"Therefore, if the whole church comes together in one place, and all speak with tongues, and there come in those who are uninformed or unbelievers, will they not say that you are out of your mind?" (1 Corinthians 14:23)

One additional situation has been suggested, where speaking in tongues, followed by an interpretation would, in all probability, make sense.

That situation would be where a gathering of believers is worshipping and praising God and will, generally be making a lot of noise in the process, as we highlighted in Chapter Thirty-Three, 'The Power of Praise'.

If a prophecy was to be delivered in that situation, then a good proportion of the utterance will be lost, before the general noise dies down!

However, an inspired message, delivered in tongues, would be a signal to everyone, that there is a message from the Lord, about to be delivered. The congregation will then have time to quiet down so that the ensuing interpretation will be heard by everyone.

In that situation, you can see that speaking in tongues, with an interpretation, serves the same purpose and function as a prophetic message.

So, in these last three chapters, we have covered all the Gifts of the Spirit, as overviewed by Paul.

Let us each prayerfully, but confidently, reach out in prayer and faith to the Holy Spirit and ask for guidance and direction on what steps we should take next.

The gifts of the Holy Spirit are of supreme importance in the Church for it is how the Holy Spirit makes known the will and purpose of God to the Body of Christ and individual believers.

Each gift of the Holy Spirit played a vitally important role in the early Church, and those same gifts are of equal importance in today's Church.

This is why Paul, in particular, urges us all to "desire earnestly the best gifts".

> "So, seeing that you are zealous of spiritual gifts, seek that you may excel to the edifying of the church." (1 Corinthians 14:12)

## CHAPTER FORTY-SIX

# Healing

O ne of the clearest indications of God's love for his people is concerning healing.

If there's one aspect of Jesus' ministry, that is extremely high visibility, was his consistent compassion for those people who were sick and in physical pain.

In Chapter Forty-Three, 'The Gifts of the Holy Spirit,' we saw that healing was described in the plural, 'gifts'.

This plurality reflects that there are various kinds of physical, emotional, psychological, and mental sicknesses and signals that God's love and healing power, covers all of them.

One of the major reasons for Jesus being sent to earth was to demonstrate the will and love of the Father for His people.

> "Jesus said to them, "My food is to do the will of the one who sent me and to complete his work."
> (John 4:34)

He reaffirmed this again:

> "For I have come down from heaven not to do my own will but the will of the one who sent me."
> (John 6:38)

So, when we see him consistently healing the sick and the suffering, we know that He is demonstrating the true will and purpose of God.

In Matthew, we particularly see His love and compassion in action:

> "So, a report about him (Jesus) spread throughout Syria. People brought to him all who suffered with

> various illnesses and afflictions, those who had sei-
> zures, paralytics, and those possessed by demons,
> and he healed them." (Matthew 4:24)

> "...... he (Jesus) saw the large crowd, and he had
> compassion on them and healed their sick." (Mat-
> thew 14:14)

These are just two examples of many, where Jesus healed the sick and in so doing demonstrated the will and purpose of God for his people.

So, Jesus fulfilled the prophecy of Jeremiah, in bringing healing and deliverance to Israel:

> "For I will restore health unto thee, and I will heal
> thee of thy wounds, saith the Lord; because they
> called thee an Outcast, saying, this is Zion, whom
> no man seeketh after." (Jeremiah 30:17)

Something that is rarely mentioned in commentaries, is that there is no record of Jesus ever being sick himself.

He was never in a position where he could not fulfill the will and purpose of God, because of any physical ailment, neither were the disciples ever physically incapacitated, and not able to support the ministry of Jesus.

So, we can see that physical healing was pervasive throughout Jesus' earthly ministry and completely affirmed that Jesus' message and ministry were a true reflection of the will and purpose of God.

As if to confirm the magnitude of Christ's ministry, John makes this astounding statement about the things that Jesus did:

> "There are also many other things which Jesus did.
> Were every one of them to be written, I suppose
> that not even the world itself could contain the
> books that would be written." (John 21:25)

If we simply observe the ministry of Jesus, then being healed and healthy, is a true manifestation of the love of God, which we are all encouraged, to embrace by faith.

So, what of healing after Jesus had ascended back to heaven? What do we know about healing, as part of the Gospel, preached by the early Church?

We do know, that during his earthly ministry Jesus, had declared to his disciples:

> "Most assuredly, I say to you, he who believes in Me, the works that I do he will do also; and greater works than these he will do, because I go to My Father" (John 14:12)

We know the reason Jesus went back to the Father, was so that the Holy Spirit could then be sent to empower the disciples to preach the complete Gospel, So, following Pentecost, we should see some compelling evidence of how that Gospel was delivered and what role, if any, healing played as an inclusive part of that message.

Let us look at three examples, each featured in the book of the Acts:

> "And believers were increasingly added to the Lord, multitudes of both men and women so that they brought the sick out into the streets and laid them on beds and couches, that at least the shadow of Peter passing by might fall on some of them" (Acts 5:15)

> "Now God worked unusual miracles by the hands of Paul, so that even handkerchiefs or aprons were brought from his body to the sick, and the diseases left them, and the evil spirits went out of them." (Acts 19:12)

> "And it happened that the father of Publius lay sick of a fever and dysentery. Paul went into him and prayed, and he laid his hands on him and healed him. So, when this was done, the rest of those on the island who had diseases also were healed" (Acts 28:9)

So, evidence enough that physical healing was an integral part of how the early Church delivered the Gospel of Jesus Christ and physical healing was as pervasive in the ministry of the early

Church as it was during Jesus' ministry.

So, what of today?

It is one of the saddest aspects of today's church environment that, in the main, healing is not regularly preached or demonstrated as part of the Gospel message.

It would appear that physical healing is many times viewed with suspicion, like some kind of "hocus pocus," rather than how the Scriptures declare it. The Scriptures declare it as a powerful gift of God's love and compassion as demonstrated, clearly and consistently, by Jesus and by the early Church.

Has God stopped loving? Has the Gospel message changed from the Bible days? Is Jesus' ministry radically different now than when He was on earth?

Of, course not! So, how can we access physical healing today?

There are at least three different ways in which healing is to be made available to the Church, and beyond, to non-believers also.

Firstly, healing needs to be restored as an inclusive part of the full Gospel message, precisely as it was in Jesus' ministry and clearly in the activities of the early Church.

Ministers and evangelists alike, need to upgrade their Gospel message, without delay, and incorporate healing into that message.

Secondly, healing is also a gift of the Holy Spirit as we saw in Chapter Forty-Four.

Believers are exhorted by Paul to "to desire earnestly the best gifts" of which healing is such a gift.

Those believers who have an inherent compassion for the sick, need to reach out by faith and take this gift from the Holy Spirit, and begin ministering to and praying "the prayer of faith" with sick people, expecting God to heal them.

The third route to healing is highlighted very specifically by James:

> "Is anyone among you sick? Let him call for the elders of the church, and let them pray over him, anointing him with oil in the name of the Lord. And the prayer of faith will save the sick, and the Lord will raise him up. And if he has committed sins, he will be forgiven." (James 5:14-15)

So, we see that the will of God is perfectly clear in the area of healing.

It is both a part of our inheritance as believers and yet another important way in which God displays his great love for his own people, and beyond into the unsaved world.

Let us embrace the full Gospel of Jesus Christ and be fully aware that that healing of our bodies has been catered for by Christ's great sacrifice for us:

> "But He was wounded for our transgressions, He was bruised for our iniquities; the chastisement for our peace was upon Him, and by His stripes we are healed." (Isaiah 53:5)

## CHAPTER FORTY-SEVEN

# Speaking in Other Tongues

**I**f there is ever a subject that is likely to spark controversy among Christians, it is the subject of speaking in other tongues.

We covered the gift of tongues in Chapter Forty-Four, however, it is important to go a little deeper into the purpose of tongues, both from its use in a gathering of believers, but, also to its more personal use which is connected directly, to our communion with God.

Let us review some of our insights about 'speaking in other tongues', that we looked at earlier.

The phrase "speaking in (other) tongues" is mentioned around twenty times in the New Testament, mainly by Paul and primarily to the church at Corinth.

The Greek word, used for 'tongues' is 'glossa' meaning 'a language, specifically one naturally 'unacquired.' 'Unacquired' means 'not acquired or gained,' so it's not a language that is known to the speaker, and is not learned naturally, over time, or by linguistic education.

Jesus, speaks about tongues:

> "These signs will follow those who believe: In My name they will cast out demons; they will speak with new tongues." (Mark 16:17)

Mark also uses the same Greek word, 'glossa.'

So, speaking in other tongues is a supernatural ability that enables believers to speak fluently in a language that has been not acquired through natural learning or through an academic process.

The first clear example of believers speaking in other tongues is on the day of Pentecost.

In Jerusalem, the first Christian believers, filled with the promised Holy Spirit, spoke in other tongues:

> "......and they were all filled with the Holy Spirit and began to speak in other tongues, as the Spirit enabled them to speak." (Acts 2:4)

Notice that these are languages that have been "enabled by the Spirit."

We see that they are known languages, but spoken by unlearned men, just as Jesus had prophesied.

How do we know?

> "They were all amazed and marvelled, saying to each other, "Are not all these who are speaking Galileans? How is it that we hear, each in our own native language? Parthians, Medes and Elamites, residents of Mesopotamia, Judea and Cappadocia, Pontus and Asia, Phrygia and Pamphylia, Egypt and the regions of Libya near Cyrene, and visitors from Rome, both Jews and proselytes, Cretans, and Arabs—we hear them speaking in our own languages the mighty works of God." (Acts 2:7-11)

This supernatural phenomenon is then repeated in Caesarea and Ephesus:

> "All the believers of the circumcision who had come with Peter were astonished because the gift of the Holy Spirit had been poured out even on the Gentiles. For they heard them speaking in other tongues and magnifying God" (Acts 10:46)

> "When Paul had laid his hands on them, the Holy Spirit came on them, and they spoke in other tongues and prophesied" (Acts 19:6)

Paul later explains, in his letter to the Corinthian church, the overall purpose of speaking in tongues.

He reflects on Isaiah's prophecy:

> "With men of other tongues and other lips I will

speak to this people; but even then, they will not hear Me, says the Lord. So, tongues are for a sign, not to believers, but to unbelievers" (1 Corinthians 14:21-22)

So, this supernatural gift of speaking in tongues is provided by the Holy Spirit to impact unbelievers in their own language, as was the case in Jerusalem on the day of Pentecost.

However, Paul also points to the gift of speaking in tongues as having another important application and one that is more directed at the speaker, rather than the listener.

Paul, explains:

"For he who speaks in an unknown tongue does not speak to men, but to God. For no one understands him, although, in the spirit, he speaks mysteries" (1 Corinthians 14:2).

We see that speaking in tongues is not just about impacting unbelievers in their language but also about the speaker, from their spirit, communicating directly with God.

We should note here that the unknown tongue could well be a language, which is not an earthly language.

Paul does mention, albeit briefly, 'the tongues of men and angels' (1 Corinthians 13:1).

In light of this, many believers consider that the unknown language could be a heavenly, angelic language, as well as an earthly language.

So, to what end would the gift of tongues be used to communicate directly and personally with God, rather than in a very public environment?

Paul explains in simple terms:

"He who speaks in an unknown tongue edifies himself" (1 Corinthians 14:4)

The Greek word for 'edify' is 'oikodomeō 'which means 'to increase or strengthen something'.

It's a word that was commonly used in the construction world, hence the word 'edifice'.

Paul encourages us to speak in an unknown tongue, as well as our normal tongue, as a form of personal prayer, in order to build ourselves up spiritually and draw closer to God.

So, he summarises our two prayer options:

> "What is it then? I will pray with the spirit, and I will pray with the understanding" (1 Corinthians 14:4).

Prayer with my normal tongue, engages my understanding.
Prayer in unknown tongue, engages my spirit.
Paul simply explains,

> "For if I pray in an unknown tongue, my spirit prays, but my understanding is unfruitful" (1 Corinthians 14:14).

So, today speaking with tongues has really important value to every believer, especially on a personal level.

It is clearly a means of personal edification as well as potentially making an impact on unbelievers in their own language.

So, we can now see why this simple exhortation of Paul is still relevant today:

> "I desire that you all speak in tongues" (1 Corinthians 14:5)

www.ingramcontent.com/pod-product-compliance
Lightning Source LLC
Chambersburg PA
CBHW060508130626
46553CB00002B/433